MICHAEL CHASE

A Reflective Journey

Before the Blast, Beyond the Fear & Back to Purpose

Copyright © 2025 by Michael Chase

All rights reserved. No part of this publication may be reproduced, stored or transmitted in any form or by any means, electronic, mechanical, photocopying, recording, scanning, or otherwise without written permission from the publisher. It is illegal to copy this book, post it to a website, or distribute it by any other means without permission.

Michael Chase asserts the moral right to be identified as the author of this work.

Designations used by companies to distinguish their products are often claimed as trademarks. All brand names and product names used in this book and on its cover are trade names, service marks, trademarks and registered trademarks of their respective owners. The publishers and the book are not associated with any product or vendor mentioned in this book. None of the companies referenced within the book have endorsed the book.

First edition

This book was professionally typeset on Reedsy.
Find out more at reedsy.com

For Makena.

Everything I am and everything I will ever be is rooted in the gift of being your dad.

Contents

Acknowledgments		iii
Introduction		1
1	When the World Felt Big	4
2	Kindness is a Lifestyle	8
3	She Carried the Rest	10
4	Big Brothers are the Best Brothers	14
5	The Other Half of Home	20
6	Northshore Academy	25
7	More Than Just a Game	29
8	The Long Path to the Badge	33
9	Patriot's Day	37
10	Marathon Monday	39
11	Resilience Unveiled	43
12	The Fallout	47
13	From Fear to Justice	52
14	Path to the Uniform	56
15	Patrol	62
16	Back to School	68
17	One Week. One Mission.	73
18	The Missing Piece	77
19	The Quiet Hero	80
20	Fatherhood & Purpose	84
21	Sully	88
22	Magnet	91

23	Still Standing	96
About the Author		99

Acknowledgments

This book would not exist without the people who stood with me when life split open.

To my family, for never letting me forget where I came from.

To my brother, Brad, for being my first protector and my constant reminder of humor, grit, and loyalty.

To my mom, Lynne, and my stepdad, Jim, for literally everything.

To my dad, Stu, and my stepmom, Cindy, for your steady support and encouragement throughout my journey in life. You have reminded me, gently and often, to look to the Lord when I am searching for direction. I am still finding my footing in that journey, but I know it would not have started without you.

To my daughter, Makena, whose strength, light, and love guide me every single day.

To Casey, and to Chase and Mia, thank you for filling my life with love, laughter, and so much more.

To my brothers in blue - Justin, Eric, and Steve, thank you for helping guide me as the "new old guy" on the job. Your patience and mentorship made all the difference. Be safe.

To Brandon, who fights his own battles and carries his own weight, yet still picks up the phone, still checks in, still jumps on a plane, and always reminds me that we are not meant to do any of this alone. Everyone needs someone like that in their corner. I am lucky enough to have him in mine.

To Tara, who calls me her BLG, Best Little Girlfriend, thank you for your loyalty, laughter, and for sticking with me through the hard stuff. You keep me laughing, call me out when I need it, and remind me that friendship can be both ridiculous and real at the same time.

To the staff of Essex Tech and to my colleagues at Northshore Academy, thank you for reminding me that the badge and the classroom are at their best when they build bridges.

To the survivors and families of the Boston Marathon bombing, your courage continues to shape my life and my purpose.

And to every student who has ever sat in my office, trusted me with your story, or let me walk beside you through pain, you are the reason I do this work.

Introduction

Fifteen Feet

Sulfur. Smoke. Blood. Fire.

It wasn't just in the air, it *was* the air. It coated my tongue, filled my lungs, clung to my skin. A sharp, metallic sting that settled in the back of my throat and told me, in no uncertain terms, that nothing would ever be the same again.

Just moments before, I had been standing on the restaurant's sun-soaked patio, taking in one of my favorite days of the year, Patriots' Day. Boston was alive. Joyful. The rhythmic clatter of cowbells and the roar of the crowd pulsed through Boylston Street as runners made their final push toward the finish line. It was a scene of celebration, of triumph, of community.

And then...

The world shifted.

A violent blast tore through the afternoon. A white-hot wall of pressure and sound. The kind of sound that doesn't echo, it *erases*. The ringing in my ears took over. The smoke stole the sky. The ground felt unstable, like gravity had momentarily let go of everything. My jacket lifted from my back. Shards of glass and twisted metal danced through the air.

I was fifteen feet from the second bomb.

Close enough to see the nails and ball bearings. Close enough to feel the heat on my face. Close enough to run toward it, not away.

And I did.

Not because I'm fearless. Not because I had a plan. Because when the world breaks open like that, you don't think. You move.

You grab a belt and make a tourniquet.

You press your knee into a stranger's wound.

You carry a child whose leg is gone.

You hand off a man's arm to someone with gauze.

You kneel in blood that isn't yours and hold pressure, because that's the only thing holding someone together.

The screaming didn't sound human. It sounded like what pain would say if it had a voice. I couldn't hear myself think over the sirens, the shouting, the blur of desperate voices crying out for help, for answers, for someone to do something.

So I did something.

I moved through the smoke, searching for whoever needed me next. And in that chaos, something strange happened, I found calm. Not peace, not comfort, just this razor-sharp clarity, like my body knew exactly what to do before my mind could catch up.

There was no fear. No hesitation. Just motion. Just instinct. Just the next right thing.

And when the dust began to settle, and the images started to fix themselves in my memory like photographs I didn't ask for, one question rose above the rest: *Was this how it ends?*

It wasn't.

But something did end that day.

Because the distance that mattered most wasn't those fifteen feet between me and the blast.

It was the distance between who I had been

And who I would now have to become.

The path forward would take me through trauma and triumph, through silence and sirens, through heartbreak, divorce, fatherhood, faith, and

INTRODUCTION

forgiveness. And, finally, love and the kind of happiness that comes when you've fought hard to find peace.

This isn't just a story about what happened on Boylston Street.

It's about what happened *after*.

It's about the scars you can't see.

The people who show up when the world falls apart.

And the long road back to yourself.

What follows isn't always pretty.

But it's real.

And if you've ever been knocked flat, felt lost, or questioned how you'd make it through...

I promise, you're not alone.

Let's go back to the beginning.

Let's find out how I got here.

1

When the World Felt Big

The Monsters, the Fire, and the Story I Never Let Go Of

I was five years old when I first told the story.
Two monsters came from the sky.
One was scaly and green, with curled ram-like horns and bloodshot eyes that spun in different directions. The other had glowing blue goggles for eyes and a mouth ringed with blazing fire. Its whole body looked like some twisted sea creature dipped in gasoline. They hovered behind the steeple of my preschool, the South Church in Peabody, MA, and they lit everything up. Flames leapt from the bushes, thick smoke choked the air, and the sky filled with the kind of noise only a five-year-old can hear.

I said kids were trapped inside.
And that I ran in.
Through the fire.
Past the monsters.
And out again.
Carrying the ones who couldn't get out themselves.
I didn't flinch when I told it.

Didn't stammer.

Didn't smile.

I am told I delivered the story like it was a fact. Like it had already made the rounds on the evening news.

And I believed it. Every word.

There's a photo from around that same time, me on a plastic three-wheeled motorcycle, "Traffic Patrol" stamped across the front like I had jurisdiction over the entire block. I'm wearing a plastic helmet a little too big for my head, with cowboy boots on, like I was headed for work, and a face so serious you'd think I was mid-shift. My brother is next to me, standing on his bicycle with one hand on the handlebar and the other resting on his hip like he already knew he was the cooler one. And right between us sits a shaggy dog, perfectly posed and looking dead ahead like he understood the assignment.

We didn't even know the dog's name.

We weren't allowed to have one growing up.

So we borrowed the neighbor's for the photo.

That picture wasn't staged. That was real. That was me.

Even then, I wasn't just playing, I was preparing.

To move.

To protect.

To respond.

I used to look at that photo and see a kid pretending.

Now I look at it and see a kid trying to become something.

Trying to *be* something.

Back then, I didn't know what trauma was.

Didn't know about terrorism or grief or survivor's guilt.

Didn't know how memory works, or how it doesn't.

But I knew I wanted to be brave.

I knew I wanted to help.

I knew I wanted to run *into* something when everyone else was running away.

Maybe I invented the monsters.

Maybe I didn't.

But something real lived inside that story. Something bigger than fire or fangs. I was just a little kid in a world that sometimes felt terrifying. And like most kids, I made sense of it the only way I knew how, by turning fear into purpose. By turning uncertainty into action.

It might've started as a dream. A flash of smoke outside the church. A siren in the distance. A news story overheard from the couch. Who knows. What matters is how deeply it embedded itself into me. It wasn't a passing thought. It was a seed.

I wanted to be the kid who ran into the fire.

I wanted to carry people out.

I never told that story again, not with the same conviction. The adults smiled too politely, like they didn't quite know what to do with it. My mom asked me where I had seen something like that, and I remember shrugging. Not because I was hiding anything, because I didn't know.

It had just... *been* there.

Waiting.

And then, years later, it came back. In a different kind of fire.

April 15, 2013.

Two more monsters.

Smoke again.

Screams again.

But this time, there *were* bodies.

This time, there *was* blood.

This time, I *did* run in.

I was fifteen feet from the second bomb when it exploded on Boylston Street. The heat. The ringing. The chaos. I moved toward it before I even had time to think. Toward the blast. Toward the bodies. Toward the horror.

And suddenly I wasn't five anymore.

I wasn't playing pretend.

This wasn't a church near the mall. This was a war zone in the middle of Boston. The monsters weren't in the smoke anymore, they were in the aftermath. In the disbelief. In the silence that followed the screaming.

But I wasn't frozen.

I was already moving.

And that's when I knew: maybe the story I told as a kid wasn't fiction after all.

Maybe it was a truth I hadn't yet lived.

Maybe it wasn't about monsters or fire or saving preschoolers, it was about identity.

It was about instinct.

It was about purpose.

Maybe the kid on the motorcycle always knew who he was.

And he was just waiting for the world to catch up.

2

Kindness is a Lifestyle

Strength From Him. Heart From Her.

I come from people who serve.

My dad wore the badge. My mom wore the scrubs. And long before I ever stepped into a classroom, a squad car, or stood on a stage, I was already being shaped by the quiet rituals of their everyday lives.

My father still puts on the uniform. Seventy-six years old and technically retired twice, but you'd never know it. His brass is still polished, his boots still shined, and when he walks into work like he's walking a beat, people still nod. Still notice. He's that kind of man. Six-foot-four. Shoulders square. Jaw set like stone. A presence that doesn't just walk into a room, it commands it.

When I was little, I swore he was ten feet tall. Maybe he still is.

Watching him leave the house felt like watching someone go off to war, or into purpose. His duty wasn't just to the badge, it was to an idea. That we protect those who can't protect themselves. That we show up. That we stand firm when others run. He didn't say those words out loud. He didn't need to. He lived them.

But presence comes in different forms.

My mother didn't have a siren, a take home car, and her uniform was different. But she saved lives all the same. Nurse. Calm hands. Kind eyes. No nonsense.

She came home to two boys and a house that leaned heavy with need. My father was gone a lot. Sometimes for work. Sometimes because of the bottle. And eventually, he was gone for good.

Still, she kept that door cracked, giving us permission to love him anyway. She taught kindness not with speeches, but by showing up. Again and again. For her patients. For her sons. For anyone who needed her.

They didn't raise me with lectures. They raised me with example. One taught me to be strong. The other taught me to lead with heart.

Some days I lead with one. Some days, the other. But most days, I carry them both.

Kindness is a lifestyle. And it started with them.

3

She Carried the Rest

She Didn't Need Applause

My mother didn't march through life like she was owed anything. She moved like someone who had already paid in full. Not loud. Not flashy. But unstoppable.

Greek by blood. Nurse by trade. Caregiver by instinct.

She made life feel full even when it wasn't fair. Lemon chicken and potatoes on a Tuesday night. A handwritten note in my lunchbox. A hug that lasted a second too long because she knew I needed one more breath of safety before stepping into the chaos of the world.

She gave and gave and gave. And when you thought she was tapped out, she somehow found a little more.

I don't remember her ever sitting still. She worked nights when we were young, then switched to days when we began to grow and Dad was no longer around. She held parent meetings, paid the bills, helped with homework, and covered for my father when he didn't show. She'd fold laundry and do the ironing as I laid on the couch as a seven year old, while we watched Larry Bird on the TV in the living room after another long day at work. She wasn't a superhero. She was better. She was real.

My mother's father passed from cancer when I was just six months old. I never knew him, but the stories built a picture of a fair-skinned, blue eyed, Greek man who could fix anything with his hands. A carpenter. Strong. Reserved. Humble. Caring. Loving. My mother adored him. She loved his gentleness, his patience, the way he made family feel safe. There were station-wagon trips to the drive-in and family gatherings with cousins and extended family with more food than needed. Losing him while she was becoming a mother herself shaped her in ways I think even she didn't see. She learned early that life doesn't wait for the timing to be right.

Her mother, Nana Banana, was the definition of warmth. I gave her the other nickname "Main Squeeze" when I was eight, and it stuck for the rest of her life. She led with laughter and lived for her family. She was perfume and coffee, solitaire and phone calls that could fill an afternoon. She wore gold jewelry like armor and carried love in everything she did.

Nana Banana married twice, both times to Greek men who couldn't have been more different. Papou John was quiet and steady. Papou Peter, her second husband, was loud, funny, and impossible to miss. He was the only grandfather I truly knew on that side, and he filled the role with style.

We watched the Patriots, Celtics, and Red Sox together. He'd rest his eyes for the middle innings, then wake up ready to rally for the ninth. He was quick with a joke, sometimes one a kid shouldn't hear. He told me to keep my "pecker in my pants" when I was six, and I thought he caught me peeing behind the shed while playing hide n seek. Nope. Life lessons. His humor was outrageous, but his love was real.

My Main Squeeze loved sports just as much. She'd buy me baseball and football cards, take me to card trading shows, and we'd bet on NFL games every Sunday. Win or lose, a greeting card arrived with cash in the mail each week. She wasn't a great bookie. We had cousins that handled that.

When I was nine, Nana and Papou picked me up from an All-Star baseball game for what they called a "Mystery Trip". I jumped into the back of their Cadillac with grass still on my cleats. My cousin Jenny was along for the adventure. Next stop: Toronto. They took us to the SkyDome for a Blue Jays game and to Niagara Falls. That was them. Always ready for the next adventure. My mom almost died when she got the call from north of the border. She assumed they were taking me someplace like Cape Cod. Not those two. Surprise!

They wintered in Marco Island, and every year my mom, brother, and I would fly down. Days on the beach searching for shells, nights filled with laughter and card games. They made life feel like a vacation, even when it wasn't easy at home.

My grandmother passed during my sophomore year at East Carolina University. We got the news at Thanksgiving that she had a brain tumor, and she was gone the day after Christmas. I was far from home and had no idea how to carry that kind of loss. It broke me. She was one of my constants, and suddenly she was gone.

My mother came from people who loved hard. She took the best parts of each of them and wove them into her own kind of strength. From her father she carried humility. From her mother she learned compassion and love. From Peter she inherited humor and he unknowingly taught her patience.

So when life demanded more from her than it should have, she already had the tools. She worked, provided, and protected. She never complained. When my father's absence left gaps, she filled them quietly and kept moving forward.

When the marriage fell apart, it didn't explode. It dissolved in silence. She never spoke ill of him, even when she could have. She let us hold on to the parts of him we still needed. That kind of grace doesn't come from weakness. It comes from wisdom.

As a kid, I thought she had it all figured out. As an adult, I see she was figuring it out in real time and still showing up. That's real power.

Even now, as a grandmother, she's the one who shows up first and stays last. The one who remembers every birthday, every story, every favorite snack. Especially the ice cream. Her love has no expiration date.

She taught me that kindness doesn't have to be loud. It just has to be consistent. That service isn't a job. It's a mindset. And that sometimes the bravest thing a person can do is stay soft in a hard world.

My father wore a badge and taught me to be strong.

My mother wore scrubs and taught me to love anyway.

The older I get, the more I realize that everything good in me started with her.

She didn't need applause. She just needed a reason to keep giving.

And we were it.

4

Big Brothers are the Best Brothers

Part Myth Maker, Part Big Brother, All Heart

In the fall of 1976, three years before I showed up, Brad arrived by setting the tone, the rules, and the pace for what it meant to be a Chase. By the time I came along, he had already claimed his stake as the firstborn, and according to him, I was delivered to our doorstep in a basket by a band of soccer-playing Gypsies. He still tells that story. Claims he opened the door himself and brought me in. Classic Brad. Part myth maker, part big brother, all heart.

We fought constantly growing up. Not the soft sibling squabbles you see in sitcoms. Ours were the full-contact, furniture-moving kind. We had two rules: no face, no groin. Everything else? Fair game. And despite my best efforts, I never won. Not once. Brad saw to that. He was relentless, strong, and just a little bit mean, but always in a way that felt like training. Like he was preparing me for something. And he probably was.

Because Brad's always been a fighter. Even as a kid, he had a scrappy edge to him. He wasn't the loudest or the flashiest, but when it came to defending his little brother or holding his ground, he never backed down.

He still hasn't. That protective instinct, it's just part of his wiring.

But Brad wasn't just a brawler. He was layered. As a kid, he was quieter than you'd expect. He liked nature. He had a small circle of friends. While some kids were out setting off firecrackers or stealing candy bars, Brad was just as likely to be inside watching a documentary on wolves. My mother used to beg him to be more social. He didn't care. He was content with who he was.

He had the talent to be a great athlete, but he never chased the spotlight. In Little League, he dreaded the ball being hit to him, even though he could make the play just fine. He preferred right field, the loneliest spot on the diamond, not because he lacked skill, but because it got the least attention. That was Brad. Later, he moved behind the plate and found his rhythm as a catcher. Hidden behind a mask, doing the quiet work. That's where he shined.

Brad's proudest sports moment? Winning the District 15 Championship with his 12-year-old all-star team. He got a bright blue jacket with stitched lettering and wore it like a badge of honor until it ended up buried in a box in the basement. These days, after a few drinks, he'll sneak down and throw it on again, even if it barely fits. The sleeves stop at his elbows now, but the pride still fits just fine.

Unlike me, Brad didn't love to compete. While I was talking trash to classmates before Little League games, Brad couldn't even tell you who we were playing. He didn't care. He wasn't there for the win. He was there for the ice cream afterward.

That contrast showed up again during travel soccer. Brad made the top team in town, surrounded by kids with dreams of college scholarships. But it wasn't his scene. He begged our mom to let him drop two levels down to the C team, just so he could play with kids who didn't cry after a loss. And he was thrilled. I never understood it. I still don't. But looking back, maybe he had something figured out.

Brad bloomed late, but once he did, he found his stride. By senior year, he broke out of his shell. He had friends from every circle, made people laugh without trying, and carried himself with a magnetic mix of goofball charm and big-hearted loyalty.

But underneath all of that, every prank, every joke, every awkward dinner-table moment, was the same Brad who would drop everything when someone he loved needed him.

One of the clearest examples came on a snowy morning when we were about ten and twelve. We woke up early, hoping school would be canceled, eyes glued to the bottom of the TV screen. When our district popped up, we cheered like lunatics. Mom made cocoa, and we bundled up in snow gear that took twenty minutes to put on. Then we charged into the backyard with our sleds, ready to conquer the hill we knew like the back of our hands.

We spent hours out there. Run after run, crashing and laughing, trying to outdo each other. Eventually, I was gassed, but I didn't want to admit it. So I got creative. On what I planned to be my final run, I took a dive at the bottom of the hill. Full drama. I moaned, lay flat, sold the injury hard. Brad came running. Concerned, panicked even. He hoisted me onto the sled and dragged me up the hill with everything he had. The second we hit the top, I leapt off, completely fine, and sprinted inside, laughing. I'd gotten him back for a thousand jump scares.

But karma moves fast.

Later that afternoon, I convinced him to head back out. He hesitated, but he went. On my first run, I hit a rock buried in the snow. This time, I wasn't faking. Pain shot through my leg. I couldn't stand. Couldn't breathe.

Brad didn't wait. He ran to me, helped me onto the sled, and pulled me all the way back to the house, quiet, and focused. No jokes. No complaints. Just his little brother in pain, and him doing what he always did, showing up.

It turned out I'd chipped my kneecap. Brad never mentioned the earlier prank. Never gave me grief. Just helped me, like he always had.

That day stuck with me. Because it wasn't the pain or the fall I remembered, it was Brad's face. The worry. The effort. The way he carried me without needing thanks or recognition. He's done that again and again over the years, in ways big and small.

When he started at UMass Amherst, I helped move him in. Our mom had put together a care package with snacks, a calling card, and, of all things, a box of ribbed condoms. Not exactly her style, but it was 100% Brad's. He held them up, deadpan: "Ribbed for her pleasure? I wear them inside out, for mine." He had everyone in stitches. That's him. Completely inappropriate, totally hilarious, and somehow still the glue that holds everything together.

His sense of humor is legendary, and also... dangerous. At a family dinner party once, he told a story that ended with a punchline so outrageous it cleared the room. Literally. People stood up mid-meal, grabbed their coats, and walked out into a snowstorm. That was the last time we saw those families. I call it The Last Supper. He still laughs about it. So do I. We might be the only ones.

Years later, when the bombs went off on Boylston Street and the world tilted sideways, Brad was already on the move, trying to get to me. He fought through chaos, blocked-off streets, and a panicked city, because that's who he is. He's always been that guy. The one who shows up.

And when life came for me in a different way, quietly, painfully, through the unraveling of a marriage, Brad was there again. No sirens, no spotlight. Just a house key, a guest room, and a family that took me in like I'd never left. I lived with him and his wife and their kids while I tried to sort out the mess, while I figured out how to start over. They made space for me, emotionally and physically, and never once made me feel like a burden.

It wasn't just a roof and a bed. It was safety. It was love. And in a time when everything else felt broken, that mattered more than I could ever say.

Brad and his wife have continued to be there, not just for me, but for my daughter, Makena. She was young when so much of life felt uncertain, and they made sure she knew she was part of something steady. They've had her over for dinners, checked in on her, and found small ways to remind her she's surrounded by love. When I couldn't be everything for her, they stepped in. Not with grand gestures, but with consistency. With presence. That's what Brad does. That's who he is.

In recent years, he's joined me at the Boston Marathon finish line. Sometimes shoulder to shoulder, sometimes just behind me, but always there. That spot, once just a stretch of Boylston Street, now carries weight. Ghosts. Grief. Gratitude. It's never easy to return. No matter how many years pass, the ground still hums with memory.

But having Brad with me changes that.

He doesn't ask for much. Doesn't push me to talk if I'm not ready. He just shows up. Parks himself beside me like he's anchoring me to the earth. I know that if my knees ever buckled from the emotion, he'd catch me before I hit the bricks. That's the kind of security only a big brother can offer.

There's something unspoken in those moments. We don't need to rehash the pain or name the fear. He knows what that day did to me. And I know what it means to have him beside me now, years later, still showing up.

Some people bring flowers. Others write tributes. Brad brings himself. Steady. Present. And that's enough.

It always has been.

Brad isn't perfect. But he's mine. My first rival. My first protector. The one who made me tougher, braver, and just a little funnier. He taught me that real strength isn't always loud. It's often quiet, steady, and full of heart.

And in a world where things can change in an instant, it's comforting to know that if I ever go down hard again, Brad will be there. Rope in hand. Ready to pull me home.

5

The Other Half of Home

What Time Taught Me About Him

My father is a twin. He and my uncle used to swap classes in elementary school just to see if their teachers would notice. Sometimes they did, sometimes they didn't. It was harmless trouble, the kind that made for good stories later in life, and they told them often. I loved those stories because they showed a side of my dad I rarely saw: carefree, laughing, full of mischief instead of measured control.

He grew up in a small New England home with a mother who ran a tight ship and a father who wore his Marine posture long after he left the service. My grandmother, everyone called her "Red," was exactly that. Red hair and freckles. She kept the place spotless, her faith steady, and her opinions mostly to herself in the old Yankee way.

My grandfather was a big man, about six foot four, with shoulders that filled a doorway and hands that could cover the checkers board in one move. He wasn't much for conversation. After a game or a visit, he'd look at my grandmother and say, "You ready to go, Red?" before heading for the car. He didn't linger or make small talk. He showed love by showing up, not by staying long.

When dementia began to take him, it didn't steal his size or his strength, just his mind. He knew it was coming. In the late eighties, before we had gentler language for those things, he'd call himself "the retarded retiree," trying to joke his way through what must have been terrifying. In the end, my grandmother sat with him every day at the care facility long after he stopped recognizing her. She did what she always did. She kept showing up, steady and loyal, even when nobody could tell if it mattered.

That's the kind of woman she was. The kind who would later become "GG" to her great grand kids. When she came over to watch Makena she'd quietly clean the house when she'd nap. GG would clip pages from *Better Homes and Gardens* and leave them on the counter with ideas for new flower beds or improved patio layouts. They were small gestures that said "I love you" in her special kind of way.

My father learned a lot of that same quiet love. He just expressed it differently, or maybe not at all for long stretches of time. He had demons of his own. We all do. But I didn't start to fully see his until I was well into my twenties.

One afternoon, out of nowhere, he asked if I wanted to go for a ride. It wasn't something we normally did. No big plan, no reason given, just a ride. I got in the car without thinking much of it. Somewhere along the way, he started talking, really talking, and the man I thought I knew started to come into focus in a way I hadn't seen before. He told me pieces of his childhood, pieces that explained a lot about the choices he made later in life. What shaped him. I won't share the details because they're his to tell, but I'll never forget the weight of his voice that day. I realized I had spent years judging a story I only knew half of.

When my parents divorced, my brother and I lived with my mom. There was no every-other-weekend plan, no court schedule posted to the fridge. We just saw Dad when it worked. At the time, that bothered me. I couldn't understand why he didn't fight for equal time, why he didn't push harder to have us with him. It felt like choosing distance over presence. And maybe it was. But as I got older, I started to understand that sometimes absence isn't apathy. Sometimes it is confusion, fear, or pain wearing the wrong disguise.

As a kid, I saw him as the man with the badge. The professional. The one everyone in town seemed to respect. He coached my baseball team, stood in the dugout like he belonged there, and those were the moments I felt closest to him.

Years later, I would learn just how respected he was beyond the ball field. My father served as Chief of Police in both Danvers, Massachusetts and Wolfeboro, New Hampshire, positions that only a handful of people ever hold and ones that speak to the kind of reputation he built in his career. He was known for professionalism, for steadiness, for holding the line when it mattered. I admired that, even when I struggled to understand the man behind the uniform.

Now that I wear one myself, I see things differently. I know the toll the job can take, the long nights, the hard calls, the things you can't unsee. I know what it's like to carry home the weight of everyone else's worst day and try not to let it change the way you talk to your family. I get it now. I get to see him in a new light.

Grace takes practice.

I had begun to see my father as a man, not a mystery. But before that understanding came, there were hard years too.

The ones you don't forget, even when you try.

My dad drank. Some nights it was quiet and social, but other times it filled the house with tension you could feel in your chest. He'd sit in his old rocking chair, listening to classic rock turned up loud enough to shake the walls. The creak of a wooden chair still gets me. So does the sound of ice cubes hitting the side of a glass. Those small sounds can bring me right back to the early years when Mom was working, Dad was drinking, and Brad and I were just trying to hold on.

He wasn't always angry when he drank. Sometimes he was funny, singing along to the music, joking, full of energy. I've been told he was the life of the party in his younger days, the kind of guy everyone wanted around. But those good vibes could turn fast. Nights out with the guys sometimes ended in fights, and those stories made their way home too. Mom wasn't thrilled about that part of him.

Then one day, the drinking stopped.

When that happened, it was like two different men traded places. The one who had been loud, unpredictable, and social disappeared. The circle of friends faded away. For Brad and me, sobriety was a relief. The air in the room changed. We didn't have to wonder what kind of night it was going to be. But even as things calmed down, there was still a piece of him that seemed missing.

In that quiet space, he found faith. He started going to church, singing hymns instead of his covers by Elvis or Three Dog Night on late Saturday nights. He found a community that gave him purpose and a path that gave him peace. I've sat in those church pews and listened to him sing. He has a great voice, and there's something about watching your father use it to praise instead of drown. It's a sound that feels like redemption.

In my high school years, my dad remarried. Cindy was the woman he had been in a relationship with while my parents were still married, and that was a hard truth for a kid to process. I didn't understand how to separate the adult decisions from the pain they caused, so I put all of it on her. At that age, blame is easier to carry than confusion.

Looking back now, I can see it differently. Life is complicated. People make mistakes. I've made plenty myself. I've worked hard to rebuild a relationship with both of them that started from a broken place. Cindy has been amazing to Makena over the years. She loves her deeply, and that matters more to me than anything that happened decades ago. I can also see how difficult it must have been for her to step into our lives at such a messy time. Her love for animals, for God, for my father, and for our family is real, and it's appreciated more than she knows.

Truthfully, I don't know where my dad would be without her. They've built something strong together, rooted in faith and forgiveness. They've both encouraged me to open my heart to God, even when I wasn't ready to hear it.

Our journey as father and son hasn't been smooth. There have been weeks and months when we hardly spoke, but love doesn't always depend on daily contact. I don't doubt his love for me or for Makena. I don't doubt mine for him either.

I used to think I had him figured out. I don't anymore. The older I get, the more I realize how little any of us truly know. But what I do know is this: I love my father. I respect the man he's become, and I've learned that understanding often grows in the same soil as pain.

He's part of my story, part of my reflection, part of the reason I try to do this work the way I do.

He is, and always will be, the other half of home.

6

Northshore Academy

Messy. Raw. Real.

Northshore Academy wasn't in any brochure. You didn't find it on a college prep tour or hear about it at PTA meetings. A school designed to support students with social, emotional, and behavioral disabilities. It was the kind of place you ended up when every other door had closed. When the guidance counselor sighed. When the public school finally closed its doors sent you home for good. When the world quietly decided you were someone else's problem.

But that's not what we believed.

I started working in classrooms there. We taught the same subjects you'd find in any high school: English, math, science. But the real lessons had little to do with World Lit. We taught patience. Boundaries. Resilience. We taught students how to stay in their seats, how to walk away from a fight, how to show up again tomorrow even when today felt impossible.

Eventually, I became the Student Support Coordinator. A title that sounds clinical but really meant: Handle the hard stuff. It was part educator, part mentor, part crisis manager. I handed out break losses,

detentions, suspensions. Sat in on expulsion hearings. I kept a log of behaviors, ran debriefs after restraints, and wrote incident reports until my fingers cramped. I helped keep the building standing.
    But most importantly, I watched the kids. Closely. Every hallway. Every classroom. Every moment.
    This was the type of school where we promised parents, probation officers, and judges that we'd keep eyes on the students. No one left a classroom without an escort. Bathrooms were one in, one out. Doors stayed locked. We didn't work off a bell schedule. Every student had to be seated, every staff member in the doorway, before a class could transition. Eyes on. Every kid. Every day.
    The days were long. Some of them brutal. I restrained the same student three times in one morning. Got spit at. Cursed at. Threatened. And then got up the next day and did it again.
    But it wasn't all punishment. The break loss room, where students went when they'd lost their privilege to join the group during free time, became sacred ground. Those were my favorite moments. One-on-one. Quiet. Just me and a kid who was struggling. It's where the real work happened.
    One day, there was only one student assigned to break loss. A 15-year-old who had been circling the edge for a while. The expectation was silence. The hope? Maybe a little schoolwork. But I saw it as an opportunity: 25 minutes to sit and work on redirecting the path. A window to remind him he mattered.
    He opened the door, stepped in, and without a word, closed it behind him. I watched as he flipped the lock.
    "Put your hands up," he said. "You're about to get into a fight."
    I stood from my desk, kept my hands open and fingers up. I told him he didn't want to do this. He disagreed.
    This wasn't a tantrum. It was calculated. This kid trained in MMA. We'd talked about his fights, his coaches. He was proud of his strength.

About 5'10", 165 lbs. At 33, I was in decent shape, but I knew I wasn't about to walk away without a scrap.

He lunged. Tried to grab my shirt. I pushed off with two palm strikes to create distance. No backup was coming. Everyone else was covering the other kids on break. That policy would change after this day.

He came again, this time with a punch. A full-force right hook. I slipped it, stepped in, and took him to the ground. He tried to wrap his legs around my waist, fighting like he'd been trained to. I held my position, glanced at the door.

One of my closest friends, Ed Crowley, was staring at me from the other side of the glass. Eyes wide. Frozen. The door was locked. None of us carried keys back then. We were tenants in a public elementary school. That door was never supposed to be locked.

He ran to find another way in. Probably thought about kicking it down. Ed reminded us often that he benched 315. But even if he had the upper body strength, he didn't have the calves for it.

More staff arrived and they were able to gain access to the room. We transitioned from a fight, into a four-person restraint. The student calmed. We released. No injuries on my end. He wasn't so lucky. His parents came for a meeting later that week. That was his last day.

We hadn't argued. We weren't building toward that moment. I think he just wanted to prove something. Maybe to me. Maybe to himself.

I hope he's doing okay.

I had students who robbed banks. One who held up a convenience store with a hypodermic needle he claimed was infected with AIDS. Another lit their MCAS (a state standardized exam) test on fire in the classroom. There were home invasions. Drive-bys. Pregnancies. Stabbings. Overdoses. Some of them are in prison now. Some won't ever get out.

But there was so much more than that.

There was laughter. Growth. Recovery. Tiny victories. Students who graduated. Students who apologized. Students who hugged you before walking out the door, even when the world told them they shouldn't trust anybody.

I worked with some of the best humans I've ever known, both staff and students. People who stayed late. Who cried in their cars. Who never gave up on a kid, even when it hurt.

We didn't fix anyone. But we helped them hold on. We made it harder for them to disappear. We stood in the gap.

Northshore was loud. Messy. Raw.

But it was real.

And I carried those kids with me. Still do.

7

More Than Just a Game

Coaching When the Playbook Didn't Exist

Coaching soccer was supposed to be the relief. After long, grueling days at Northshore Academy managing crisis after crisis, tracking student safety like a hawk, and doing my best to connect with kids no one else could reach, coaching gave me a place to exhale. Danvers High was a different world. The field was where things felt steady. Predictable. Clean.

I loved the game. Still do. But it was never just about soccer. I loved watching young players compete. Loved the pregame energy. Loved the chemistry of a good team, the rhythm of a practice that just clicked. I loved winning. And I did a lot of that over my 20+ years coaching high school soccer. League titles, MVPs, Coach of the Year nods, championship banners. But none of that mattered more than when a former player, ten years after graduating, chose me as the subject of a work-based learning project about the adult who impacted their life the most. Or when a player introduced me to his family with a smile and four words that meant everything: "This is my coach."

That's the win.

In late August of 2013, just four months after surviving the Boston Marathon bombing, I was gearing up for the start of another soccer season. I had my practice plan ready. Cones, pinnies, water jugs all packed in the truck. About 60 student-athletes were set to show up at tryouts. I was ready to go.

Then the call came.

It was the Athletic Director. A new student had shown up to the wrong field. Could I swing by and pick him up? Of course. I drove the mile back to the school, parked, and met a tall, lean kid named Philip Chism. Just moved up from Tennessee. Quiet, polite. We made small talk during the ride, and I did what I could to welcome him. When we pulled into the field, I introduced him to the squad.

My teams were tight. More family than roster. And the boys treated Phil as one of their own. He had 60 brothers from day one. The kind of support that makes you feel like you belong, even in a brand-new place.

Phil played on JV and quickly stood out. Talented. Fast. Leading scorer. He was a no-brainer to be called up for the varsity tournament roster. I was proud of his progress.

Then came October 20th.

Practice that day was routine. We were in tournament mode. I told the team I'd be leaving a few minutes early to attend our league's All-Star selection meeting. As I scanned the group, I noticed Phil wasn't there. Someone said he might have stayed after for extra help. He'd been in school that day. That was all we knew.

That evening, as I sat in a classroom at a nearby high school with the other coaches, my phone rang. It was one of my captains. I let it go to voicemail. It rang again. I stepped out.

"Coach, have you heard from Phil? He didn't come to the team dinner. His mom hasn't heard from him either. We're getting worried."

They were already organizing search teams. Flashlights, carloads of teammates combing the town looking for their friend. I tried calling Phil.

Texted him. Nothing. I called a friend of mine, a detective in town. Left a message.

Around 9 p.m., he called me back.

"Mike," he said. "Tell your boys to stop looking. Phil's been found. They need to go home. I'll explain when I can."

None of us knew. None of us could have imagined.

The truth came out slowly. Philip Chism had not just disappeared. He had raped and murdered Colleen Ritzer, a beloved math teacher at the school. He had done it inside the building, while we were outside at practice. He dragged her body into the woods. A few hours later, he was found walking along Route 1 in Topsfield.

I've worked with troubled kids my whole life. I've seen what trauma and untreated pain can do. I've worked with students who committed murder. But I didn't see this coming. No red flags. No warning signs. Nothing that pointed to the darkness behind that quiet demeanor.

The days that followed were a blur of shock and sorrow. Our community was shattered. My players, especially the ones who had embraced Phil, brought him in, sat beside him on the bus and at team dinners, were gutted. They didn't just lose a teammate. They lost a sense of safety, trust, and certainty.

And once again, I was thrown into a role I never asked for. No manual. No playbook.

I showed up. That's all I knew to do. I listened. I sat with them. I helped families process what no one should ever have to explain. I didn't have answers, but I had presence. And sometimes that's all a coach can offer.

Soccer wasn't about X's and O's. It was about raising boys into men. About being a steady voice when the world around them fractured. About helping them grieve and rebuild and believe again.

What happened to Colleen Ritzer was evil. Unthinkable. And while I didn't know her personally, I carry her memory, because I knew the boy who took her life. I knew the team that took him in. I know the pain of trying to coach through that kind of storm.

There were no trophies that season. No celebration.

But we showed up.

We held each other up.

And in some ways, that season became the most important one of all.

8

The Long Path to the Badge

A Funeral that No One Came To

I told the principal at Northshore Academy not to get too attached. "I won't be here long," I said. "Just waiting for my number to be called."

It was 2001. I had just taken a job at a small, alternative high school with students who carried heavy burdens, but I was carrying one of my own, the unshakable belief that I was meant to be a cop.

In Massachusetts, that meant Civil Service. For those unfamiliar, Civil Service is a bureaucratic labyrinth with a few gates: a written exam, a ranking system, and then, the waiting. Towns choose candidates off an eligibility list, and unless someone retires, moves, dies, or screws up, there's not much movement. In 2001, the economy was steady, nobody was leaving, and everyone wanted in. Cops were still heroes. It was job security, good benefits, early retirement, and respect.

I was placed on the reserve list for the Danvers Police Department. Essentially a seat in the waiting room of your dream. Ten of us sat on that list like a pack of rookies warming the bench, uniforms imagined, not issued. The department said it was a matter of time. But time doesn't move the same in government work.

Years passed.

Northshore became less of a detour and more of a destination. I found meaning in the work, connection with the students, but the badge still tugged at me. I kept one foot in each world. Until my body forced me to slow down.

In 2004, after my third ACL reconstruction on my left knee, I felt something wasn't right. A tightness in my chest. Pain. Shortness of breath. I dismissed it at first. I had a high tolerance, maybe too high. But when I finally went to the hospital, they discovered I had pulmonary embolisms: blood clots in both lungs.

Let that sink in: both lungs.

According to the Mayo Clinic and CDC, untreated pulmonary embolisms are fatal in about 30% of cases. Even with treatment, the death rate hovers around 2 to 8 percent, depending on severity and response time.

I didn't beat the odds. I survived them. I spent nearly two weeks in the hospital, then went home on Coumadin, a blood thinner that was now my silent companion. I was 25 years old and being told to avoid alcohol, get my blood drawn weekly, and monitor my INR levels like I was a retiree in Florida, not a young man training for a badge.

I followed the rules. For six months, I was a model patient. I even came off the meds... for a while.

Then my leg ballooned. Swollen from the knee down. A quick ultrasound showed something, maybe new clots, maybe scar tissue. The doctor couldn't be sure. But his prescription was certain: Coumadin for life.

That was the first time I heard it. "For life."

In 2006, I got the call I had been waiting for. Danvers PD was sending me to the academy. I was ecstatic. I quit my coaching job. Informed the principal at Northshore Academy. I was ready to trade my lesson plans for a duty belt.

I passed the psych eval. Nailed the Physical Abilities Test. Filled out the health history paperwork like it was a golden ticket.

Then I sat across from the town's medical examiner.

He flipped through my file, nodded a few times, and then paused. He asked me about the Coumadin. I explained the situation, the clots, the hospital stay, the blood work, the lifetime prescription. He left the room.

When he returned, he was holding a massive medical book. Thick, dense, and filled with rules I didn't write.

"I'm sorry," he said, flipping to a highlighted section. "Under state and federal standards, you're classified as being under chronic anticoagulation therapy. You're disqualified from police work in every state."

I blinked. "You're telling me I can't be a cop? Anywhere?"

He didn't have to say it again.

That was it. The dream I'd chased since I was five years old, the one forged watching my father shine his brass and lace his boots, died in that sterile office under fluorescent lights and a highlighted passage in a book I'll never forget.

I tried to argue. I met with hematologists. Sought second, third, even fourth opinions. But the message never changed: you're safer on Coumadin. You're not cleared for police work.

I called Northshore Academy and got my job back. I returned to the classroom and, eventually, back to the soccer field. But I was walking around with a quiet grief no one could see. I wasn't injured. I wasn't sick. I just... wasn't allowed.

People don't talk enough about what it feels like to be disqualified from your own dream. There's no funeral. No "I'm sorry for your loss." Just an ache you carry. A uniform you never get to wear. A version of yourself you never get to become.

I stayed in education. I kept coaching. I poured myself into the work in front of me, because that's what we do when the future we imagined gets closed off. We pivot. We persist.

But if you're reading this, you already know something changed. You've seen the uniform.

That chapter's coming. The part where I fought to come off the meds, got new opinions, and clawed my way back. But that part of the story only exists because of what happened on Boylston Street in 2013.

If not for the bombs... if not for the smoke, the screams, and the aftermath... I wouldn't be writing this chapter as a cop.

But that's a story for another day.

9

Patriot's Day

More than Just a Race

There's one Monday in April that means more to me than most holidays ever could. In Massachusetts, we call it Patriots' Day. A day that commemorates the first shots of the American Revolution in Lexington and Concord. But in Boston, it has become something far deeper, far more alive.

Patriots' Day is the heartbeat of a city waking up from a long winter. After months of cold, slush, and gray skies, spring finally steps forward. The flowers begin to bloom in the Public Garden. The air softens. The Charles River glimmers under a sun we almost forgot existed. And the people of Boston? We come alive.

For me, Patriots' Day was always a ritual. Working at Northshore Academy was rewarding, but exhausting. April Vacation offered a rare pause, a moment to exhale. And every year, I used that first Monday to head into the city. Sometimes with friends, sometimes alone. But always with the same plan: find my spot on Boylston Street and just take it all in.

What I love most about the marathon isn't just the race, it's the runners. It's who they are. Early-morning joggers fitting in miles before the kids wake up. Parents pushing strollers and personal limits. People raising money and awareness for causes that changed their lives or saved someone else's. Veterans. Survivors. First-timers. Lifers. All chasing something bigger than a finish line.

It's about grit. It's about purpose. It's about doing something hard, together.

The Boston Marathon is a stage for every story imaginable. People don't just run 26.2 miles for themselves. They run for charities, for healing, for hope. They run for their late mother, for their sick child, for the hospital that pulled them through. The race becomes a megaphone for nonprofits and causes working quietly behind the scenes all year long, saving lives, changing lives, lifting up those who need it most.

And the city shows up for them. Every step of the way.

In 2013, I almost didn't go. Life was hectic. Work was draining. I was tired. But something pulled me in. Something about that day, about the people, the energy, the tradition, felt too important to miss.

So I went.

And that decision changed everything.

But even before the chaos and heartbreak that unfolded that year, Patriots' Day had always been a reminder of what matters: community, resilience, and showing up. It's a celebration of ordinary people doing extraordinary things. It's a love letter to effort. And in a world where we often see the worst of each other, Patriots' Day is a moment where we see the best.

It's more than a race.

It's who we are.

10

Marathon Monday

A Day of Celebration

April 15, 2013. Patriots' Day. Marathon Monday.

The sun cracked through the blinds like it always did, unbothered and beautiful. The kind of morning that promises something. A light breeze. Blue skies. Boston coming alive. If you've lived here long enough, you know. Marathon Monday is more than a race. It's a religion. And that day, the whole city was headed to church.

I did what I always did. Tossed on a fleece, grabbed the essentials, and made my way to the Beverly commuter rail. The train was already buzzing with life. Sox hats. Marathon jackets. Bruins gear. Strangers swapping stories like old friends. Every bench and aisle packed with people chasing the same feeling. Something big, something joyful.

Fenway had the earliest first pitch in baseball on this day each year. The Red Sox always played early so the fans could spill out and line the course. Add in a Bruins playoff game at the Garden that night and Boston wasn't just alive. It was electric. You could feel it humming in your bones.

I didn't have a plan. Just knew I wanted to get close to the finish line.

That was it. I figured I'd find a place with a patio, order a beer, and soak in the atmosphere. That's when I saw him, an old buddy from high school baseball. He was a couple rows down on the train, weaving through bodies and backpacks. He spotted me, lit up, and said his family was heading to the Atlantic Fish Company on Boylston Street. Never heard of it. Didn't matter. I said I'd meet him.

By the time I hit Copley Square, the air felt different. Charged. People were laughing. Cheering. High-fiving strangers. The kind of unity you don't see every day unless you're lucky enough to be in Boston on Patriots' Day. The Atlantic Fish Company came into view like a postcard. Outdoor patio. Packed with people. Two hundred yards from the finish line.

We posted up at a high-top table, a front-row seat to one of the most iconic stretches in sports. It was perfect. The weather kept dancing between sun and clouds. We were peeling off layers, putting them back on, sipping drinks, waving at runners. You know those days you wish you could bottle up forever? It was one of those.

Then Brad called. He and his wife, Jen, had made it to The Harp, a bar right outside the Boston Garden. They had Bruins tickets and wanted to meet up for a drink. I tried explaining the maze of streets and barricades, how to get to our side of Boylston Street. We were mid-call at 2:49 PM when everything changed.

BOOM.

I felt it in my chest before I heard it. A low thud that rattled my bones. I turned left toward the finish line and saw smoke rise like a ghost across the street. My first thought? Cannon fire. A celebration? But no. It was almost 3pm. The elite runners were long gone. Something was wrong. Brad was still on the phone. He heard it too. "What the hell was that?"

BOOM.

The second one hit fifteen feet to my left. The taste of sulfur slapped my tongue. I felt heat on my skin. The noise, louder than anything I've ever heard. Deafening. Paralyzing. The blast knocked the air out of me. But somehow, I didn't freeze.

I dove on top of two of the women from our group. Shielded them with my body. Instinct. The world around us disappeared into white smoke and ringing ears. Time slowed. Sound dropped out. And still, my brain sped up. I could feel everything. Glass raining down, fire dancing in the trees, the sidewalk shaking beneath my knees.

The human mind is wild. In the worst chaos, it can find clarity. My senses kicked into overdrive. The screaming returned, rising out of the fog. I spotted a narrow alcove between Atlantic Fish Company and the restaurant next door. It looked like safety. A small area where the utilities entered the side of the building. I got the women up and hustled them into that space, away from the street, away from more possible blasts. I stood between them and everything else.

Brad was still on the line. I hadn't hung up. He was miles away, hearing everything through a tiny speaker. I stuffed my cell phone into my back pocket. Line still open.

Through the smoke, I saw our group inside the restaurant. Panic had replaced laughter. Glass everywhere. People diving under tables. But the real horror was out on the sidewalk. People down. People bleeding. People screaming.

I told the women we had to move. Stay low. Go fast. I guided them down the patio, scanning everything. Faces. Bags. Rooftops. Every nerve firing. We pushed through the door and into the restaurant.

And then, I turned around.

I left them behind and walked straight back into hell.

I pulled the phone from my pocket, barked into it: "Get out of the fucking city. Children are hurt." Then I hung up.

Because that was the moment it all shifted.

The moment I became someone else.

The next minutes would be burned into me forever. Not just because of what I saw. But because of what I did. And what others did too. Strangers helping strangers. People ripping shirts off their backs to stop the bleeding. A thousand individual choices that stitched together the story of Boston Strong.

Love showed up.

In the middle of the carnage, kindness still had a pulse.

This wasn't the ending I expected for Marathon Monday. But maybe it was the beginning of something else. Something more powerful.

Pain was the entry point. But purpose? That was waiting on the other side.

11

Resilience Unveiled

Responding to the Chaos on Boylston Street

When I turned back to the street, the scene felt surreal and gut-wrenching. Bodies lay sprawled across the pavement, screams and moans folding into the air. A moment earlier the street had been alive with celebration, and now it felt like the world had quietly tilted and forgotten how to breathe. Carriages designed for children stood empty, stark reminders of lives abruptly disrupted. One image seared into me. A sneaker, torn away, still holding a foot. The shock hit like a cold wave, but there was no time to stop moving. The street looked like people's pockets had been turned inside out. Singed dollar bills drifted across the sidewalk. Personal belongings were scattered everywhere, as if the blast had ripped them out of the air mid-life.

Surveying the chaotic scene, a man emerged, visibly shaken, his clothes torn and singed. I moved to assist him, guiding him from the sidewalk and into the waiting arms of the compassionate waitstaff at the Atlantic Fish Company. Their dining room had been transformed into a triage unit in a matter of seconds, and the urgency to help became my only focus.

There, in the middle of the chaos, I spotted a young girl lying injured in the center of the raceway. Instinct took over. I vaulted over the metal fencing that had separated spectators from runners moments before and found myself on Boylston Street. The steady flow of the marathon had become a stampede of civilians, police, and emergency personnel all running in the opposite direction. Fear moved through the street like its own current.

Navigating the scene, my attention locked onto a six-year-old girl who was courageously facing the unthinkable. Another man was already there, doing everything he could to stabilize her. She had lost her leg from just below the knee. He asked urgently for a tourniquet. I slid off my belt and worked it under her leg, pulling it as high as I could toward her hip.

Despite the unimaginable pain she was enduring, she remained conscious and remarkably strong. Tears filled her eyes as I told her she would be okay. I promised her we were going to get her to safety.

Her father and older brother appeared beside us as we lifted her. Ambulances had been stopped from driving directly into the blast site because of the fear of a third or fourth explosion. We scooped the little girl up, and I held her leg firmly against the belt as we began the sprint toward the EMTs. The blast had ruptured my left eardrum, and the ringing made it almost impossible to hear. I encouraged the father to follow closely, keeping his son's eyes shielded from what no child should ever see.

As we reached the Prudential Center, communication was still difficult, but determination carried us forward. At the back of an ambulance, I told the father to stay with his daughter. I shifted roles and brought his oldest son to the curb on Boylston Street, a small pocket of calm where I could check him for injuries.

I started with his head and neck, then moved down. He winced and pointed to his calf. Lifting his pant leg, I saw six or eight small, perfectly circular marks beginning to bruise. The skin was unbroken. They looked like what you would expect from a BB gun fired with barely any force. None of us understood at the time that these injuries likely came from BBs packed inside the pressure cooker bombs. That realization would come later.

While I was assessing the boy, a sudden commotion erupted behind me. I turned to see a Boston Police Officer sprinting toward us, frantic and yelling. I did not yet realize that a stranger had been standing above us, recording my interaction with the boy on his phone. With countless people in need of help, he had chosen to film instead of act. The officer, offended by the disregard for the suffering around us, confronted him. The man ran, and the officer continued on. The moment revealed a strange clash of instincts in crisis. Some people ran toward helping. Others ran toward documenting.

The boy's father returned, and the reunion between them was immediate and wrenching. He pointed toward the blast site and cried out, "My son. My son." Only then did I realize there was a third child. The urgency hit me again, and I ran back into the fray.

Carnage surrounded me. Many had lost limbs, and blood covered the pavement. Yet in the darkest moments, humanity still showed itself. Strangers holding each other up. Strangers becoming lifelines.

I found the eight-year-old boy and realized he was the family's third child. Others and I worked together, doing everything we could to save him. His injuries were too severe. It was the first time in my life I had come face-to-face with death. It did not look like the movies. It looked like a little boy who never should have been there. Something in me shifted in that moment, a piece of myself I understood I would never get back.

Afterward, I stayed on scene, passing backboards, shifting barricades, and helping first responders however I could. I gave a detailed account to police officers, trying to offer anything that might help make sense of what had just happened.

At the epicenter of the blast, I found my friend from the train. We embraced, both shaken. He stood without a shirt, having given it to the mother of the young boy we could not save. She had been injured, and he had used his shirt to help control her bleeding. I took off my blood-covered quarter-zip and handed it to him. Together we walked away from what felt like a war zone, trying to find our people.

Finding anyone was nearly impossible. Thousands were fleeing, cell phone service was gone, and the city felt like it had been knocked off its axis. It reminded me of trying to meet up with friends in the nineties without a plan, except this time the stakes were life and death.

Through the thinning crowd, a figure came running toward us. It was Brad. My brother had run from Mass General, searching through the chaos for me. I still do not know how he found me. He scooped me up, and we made our way back to his vehicle.

With little said and tears shed, we left the city, stopping first at Salem Hospital for an evaluation. Sitting in the Emergency Room, I watched the footage on TV for the first time. I could not hear well enough to follow the broadcast, so I relied on the subtitles. They became my lifeline. Seeing the aerial view of the street I had just been thrown into made the truth impossible to ignore.

I had survived a terrorist attack. It was a realization that carried its own weight. Gratitude. Disbelief. And the first stirrings of understanding how fragile everything can be.

12

The Fallout

The Long Road to the Right Room

I returned to work the following Monday.
Looking back, I thought that was the right move. It felt like the right move. In reality, I was desperate to cling to a shred of normalcy. I desired the same normalcy that had been violently stripped from me just days before on Boylston Street.

The school secretary, always thoughtful, had planned a celebration in my honor. She wanted to recognize me for what I had done and what I had survived. Saving that little girl's life. Staying calm in the chaos. Being there when others couldn't. Her heart was in the right place, and I'll always appreciate that. But I knew, almost immediately, that this wasn't the way back for me. I didn't want banners or applause. I didn't want to be the hero.

I wanted Friday. The day before April break. Another "normal" day at work.

I wanted coffee in the hallway and quick check-ins with coworkers. I wanted kid updates and inside jokes. I wanted to stand in our usual morning circle, arms crossed or hands in pockets, as we passed around the same kinds of logistical details that make a school run. I wanted to pretend that nothing had changed.

But everything had.

I hadn't eaten. I was barely drinking water. I hadn't slept in days. And yet, on the outside, I looked fine. I wore the same clothes I'd worn many times before. Face clean-shaven. Head freshly buzzed. The image of who I had always been. But underneath the clothes was a shell. A body on autopilot. A mind unraveling.

No one told me how hard the silence would be. Or how loud it would get.

The celebration was postponed. I stepped into the circle like I always had, said what I needed to say, nodded where I needed to nod. And then I got back to work, sort of. At least, I tried. But that first week wasn't a return. It was a slow, quiet collapse.

I had my first flashback that week.

It happened during a restraint. The first one since I'd come back. A girl was in crisis, and I moved in instinctively, as I had so many times before. But something inside me cracked. The pressure, the physical closeness, her screams, the tension...it ignited something deep in my nervous system. It was brief, but I felt it. My first panic attack.

Days later, I was in a CPR training. Just a manikin. Just compressions. I was surrounded by familiar faces. Professionals. Colleagues I respected. And then, suddenly, I wasn't in the training anymore.

I was back in the street.

Kneeling, not on the carpet in the classroom, but on the pavement. Compressing that little boy's chest. Hearing nothing. Feeling everything. I was scooped up and dropped fifteen miles away into a moment I wasn't ready to face again. It came with a heat, like my body was on fire from the inside out. I felt faint. Disoriented. It was brief. But that was enough.

A colleague noticed. She touched my shoulder gently, said my name, and I blinked back into the classroom. I nodded like I was fine. I wasn't.

I quickly left the room and found an empty office. Opened a window. Cried like I hadn't let myself cry since the bombing. I remember looking out over the parking lot and thinking, *This is different. I'm different. Everything is different now.*

That was the moment I knew I wasn't okay. Not even close.

I needed help.

But finding help wasn't easy. Someone once told me that finding the right therapist is like shopping for jeans. Just because it looks good on the hanger doesn't mean it fits. Sometimes you have to try six or seven pairs before you find the one that works. That was exactly my experience. I met all kinds of professionals with all kinds of styles. Some were solid. Some were strange. One session, in particular, felt like an audition for a hidden camera show.

From the moment I stepped into her office, I knew we weren't going to be a fit. The room smelled like patchouli oil. She wore a full-length, flowy dress with a thin, flowered headband holding back wisps of brown hair. She looked like she had just stepped out of Woodstock. Her tone was warm, soft and somehow completely patronizing. Like I was a lost second grader who needed to find the front desk at the library.

We skimmed over the basics of what happened on Boylston Street, and she nodded solemnly. Then, just as we were approaching something real, a chime rang out to signal our time was up. That's when it got weird. She asked me to close my eyes. I cracked one open and saw that she had closed hers, hands raised slightly like she was channeling an energy force.

"Michael," she said, her voice airy and slow, "I want you to picture a box. It's a magical box. The magical box is in the corner of the room."

Both of my eyes were now open.

"Now," she continued, "I want you to take all of those terrible images and memories and stuff them in that magical box."

And I swear to God, all I could think about was a vagina. That's what "box" meant in my world. I was trying not to laugh, trying not to be rude. But I knew right then, there would be no second session. I'm sure she's helped a lot of people over the years, but I paid my copay and practically ran to the parking lot.

Eventually, though, I walked into the right office.

I knew it the second I sat down. No incense. No magical boxes. Just calm professionalism. Her approach was direct, no frills. She didn't tiptoe around the trauma. She didn't baby me. Trust was built without much effort. We got right to work. And that work began with EMDR.

EMDR stands for *Eye Movement Desensitization and Reprocessing*. At first, the name didn't mean much to me. It sounded clinical, almost sterile, like something pulled out of a psychology textbook. But what it really meant was hope. The philosophy behind it is simple in theory but powerful in practice: when something traumatic happens, your brain doesn't always file it away like a normal memory. Instead, it leaves it raw and jagged, scattered everywhere, ready to cut you without warning. EMDR gives your brain a chance to reprocess those moments, to move them from the surface where they're always burning into a place where you can carry them without being crushed.

The treatment was first used with combat veterans coming home from the Middle East, men and women carrying images of roadside bombs, ambushes, and firefights that refused to let them sleep or breathe. Many of them couldn't shut it off, couldn't get their bodies to believe they were safe even when they were home. EMDR gave them a way to turn the volume down on those memories without erasing them, to take the sting out of the flashbacks and make life livable again.

In practice, it looks simple. You hold small plastic devices, tappers, that gently vibrate in alternating rhythms between your left and right hand. That back-and-forth motion is what seems to unlock the brain's natural processing system. It sounds strange until you're in it. But when it works, it feels like someone is finally helping you carry the weight you've been dragging alone.

We started the first session after our intro by walking through the entire day. I shared everything from the moment my eyes opened to the moment I went to bed. Every detail. Every sound. Every scream. We sat together for hours. She warned me I'd be exhausted after our sessions. She was right. But I still couldn't sleep.

Not yet.

She told me that EMDR would help with that. That eventually, the exhaustion would lead to rest. That my brain just needed time to catch up. And she was right again. After a few sessions, I started sleeping. Four hours. Then six. Then eight. Sometimes I'd even nap after therapy and still sleep through the night. It was a miracle.

EMDR didn't erase my memories. That's not how it works. It doesn't make you forget. It helps you file the trauma away where it belongs, on a shelf, instead of scattered all over the floor of your mind. I could still recall what happened on my worst day, but I could finally choose when to recall it. It wasn't just showing up and hijacking my body anymore.

It was incredible work. And it saved my life.

13

From Fear to Justice

Face to Face with a Monster

There was something strange about watching it all unfold from my couch, fifteen miles north of Boston, but still feeling like the danger was just outside my door. The city had been turned into a battlefield. A manhunt was on. And the monsters I thought I'd left behind in childhood had returned. Only this time, they weren't born of preschool imagination. They were real. And they were on the loose.

I'd been holding it together, or at least pretending to. But I couldn't stop watching the coverage. My eyes glued to the screen as if the answers I needed would crawl out of the ticker tape. SWAT teams, armored vehicles, bomb squads. Cops from every corner of the state alongside federal agents, sweeping through Watertown and Boston like hunters closing in on a beast. It was surreal and terrifying. And somewhere in the middle of that chaos was a question that had been haunting me since Boylston Street: *What happened to the little girl I helped?*

Her name was Jane. I didn't know that at the time. I didn't even know if she'd survived.

In the days after the bombing, the media swarmed. Cameras parked outside my door. Anchors left voicemails. Everyone wanted the story. But I wasn't ready. I didn't want attention. I wanted connection. I needed answers.

That's when 20/20 called. Something about them felt different. Less spectacle, more substance. I said yes, not to tell my story but to find hers.

A young, sharp, and gregarious producer showed up at my brother's house. She was taking the lead, with another team member quietly in the background. She leaned in, engaging, direct, and asked me one simple question: "Do you want to find the little girl you helped?"

That was her angle. That was her pitch. She promised this interview would lead me to her. And I didn't disagree.

Soon I was in the back of a network car, heading for the Boxer Hotel in Boston, about to sit under bright lights and tell the story I had been trying to piece together in my own head.

Other survivors were there too. Each of us carrying fractured memories, trying to make sense of the worst day of our lives. For me, it wasn't about television. It was about finding the missing thread: the little girl. Who was she? Where was she? Was she okay?

After we wrapped, their car dropped me in the North End. My favorite corner of the city. A quiet dinner the producers arranged, meant to give me space. The North End is Italian through and through, almost two hundred restaurants crammed into a few blocks. The kind of place where you can't walk five steps without the smell of garlic and red sauce trailing you.

As I finished the meal and jumped back into the car, a message came in from a friend who had been digging on her own.

"It's Jane," she wrote. "The little girl you helped is Jane Richard. Martin's sister. She was wearing green."

The name hit me like a wave. Martin Richard. The boy who didn't make it.

Suddenly everything hurt again. And still, somehow, I felt lighter. The not knowing had been its own kind of torment. Now I could breathe. Just barely. I had an answer. And with it, a direction.

But while I was searching for answers, the monsters were writing their own ending.

My interview never even aired in Boston or on the East Coast. The manhunt broke into the broadcast. The brothers carjacked a man, murdered Officer Sean Collier as he sat in his cruiser, and turned Watertown into a war zone. Pipe bombs, pressure cookers, gunfire echoing through suburban streets. The older brother was killed that night, shot several times by police before being run down by the same brother he had been trying to protect.

The city went dark. Boston was locked down. Families told to stay inside. Helicopters overhead. Sirens that never stopped. The younger brother slipped away, but only for a night. By the next day, he was found hiding in a boat in someone's backyard not far from the initial firefight.

One dead. One captured. And for a moment, Boston exhaled.

The nightmare was over.

Or at least, that's what we thought.

The sentencing hearing came later. I didn't attend the trial, but I watched closely. I followed the headlines. The legal arguments. The evidence. The testimony. And then, one day, I was asked to speak.

A victim impact statement.

I sat for hours, drafting and redrafting, trying to capture something that could never truly be explained. How do you summarize the impact of almost dying? Of seeing what I saw? Of carrying it with me every single day since? I wrote the statement myself. I had to. It was mine to carry, and mine to deliver.

The morning of the hearing, my nerves were wrecked. My body felt tight. I could barely eat. The courthouse was silent when I arrived. You could feel it in the walls. The pain, the struggle, the trauma, the weight of it all. When the younger brother entered the courtroom, the sound of shackles dragging across the floor echoed like something out of a nightmare. Or a memory. I couldn't help but think of the Ghost of Christmas Past, rattling his chains. Only this was no story. This was the man who tried to kill me.

He sat just feet from me. Turned his chair. Faced me.

And we locked eyes.

He didn't flinch. Barely blinked. Showed no emotion as I cried. As I shook. As I spoke the truth he didn't deserve to hear.

But I said it anyway.

I spoke of what he did. Of who he hurt. Of how my life, and the lives of so many others, would never be the same. And I asked for one thing: that he be sentenced to death. Not out of vengeance, but out of justice. Because that's what he gave us on Boylston Street, death and destruction. I believed that's what he deserved in return.

When it was over, I sat down. And I exhaled. For the first time in a long time, I felt relief. My part was done. My truth had been spoken.

But justice has a strange way of dragging its feet.

The appeals began. Courts reversed decisions. Arguments were made. Technicalities were debated. I still get emails from the U.S. Attorney's office whenever something new happens. Invitations to join calls with legal teams explaining what's next. Sometimes I listen. Most times I don't. I've lived this story already. I don't need to hear it again.

What I do know is this: one of the monsters is dead. The other one will never be free. And I'm okay with that. I'm okay not knowing exactly when or how this ends, as long as it ends far away from here.

The monsters from my childhood came back to life that April. They didn't have scales or teeth too big for their heads. But they brought fire and fear just the same. And while I never got to slay them in some heroic battle, I did face one. I looked him in the eye. And I lived to tell the story.

Sometimes, that's enough.

14

Path to the Uniform

A Dream Deferred, But Not Forgotten

After the marathon, my therapist warned me to stop watching footage from the attacks. "Stay away from the articles, the social media posts, the conspiracy theories," she said. But I couldn't. I needed to see every video. I needed to know every detail. It consumed me.

Some called me a hero. Others, more disturbingly, called me a "crisis actor." A participant in a so-called false flag operation. I still don't know how people make up this kind of stuff and sleep at night. But it's out there. And even though I was told not to look, I did.

One day, while digging through the footage, I came across a video taken seconds after the second blast. It showed a uniformed police officer kneeling over Jane in the middle of Boylston Street, right where I found her. The video was grainy, chaotic, but unmistakable. I had no idea an officer had been with her before me. In the moment, I thought the other man and I were first to arrive. But clearly, someone had been there and left.

This isn't a judgment of that officer. I don't know what pulled him away or what decision he had to make in that moment. But seeing him there, seeing that someone in uniform was allowed to be there, while I had been told I couldn't wear the badge, lit a fire in me. Why was he considered fit for duty, and I wasn't? Why was I being told I couldn't be a cop because of a medication?

I had been on Coumadin, a blood thinner, since I developed clots after an ACL surgery. And that one medication had crushed my dream. The doctors said no. The hiring boards said no. The town's doctor said no. And yet... that fire wouldn't go out.

So I started calling my hematologist at Mass General, the guy who literally wrote the regulations on this stuff. His message was clear: "You're staying on the medication." But I'm stubborn. One of my best, and worst, traits. I kept calling. Kept pushing. Eventually, they stopped taking my calls. Maybe I was too persistent. I don't regret it.

I began seeking second opinions, then third, fourth, fifth. Most doctors deferred to the expert, my hematologist. They followed his guidance. But I didn't quit. I knew the risks. I also knew my body. No family history of clotting. All my tests were clean. I just needed one doctor to agree with me, and eventually, I found him. A cardiologist, and a few of his colleagues, saw things the way I did. They listened. We came up with a plan. I came off the medication.

Then I made the call to the Danvers Police Department. "I'm eligible," I said.

But it still wasn't smooth sailing. The new Chief, who had replaced my father when he retired and moved to New Hampshire, made it clear I wasn't his choice. For over a year, he made sure I never got hired. He too, stopped taking my phone calls. Then he retired. And one of the first calls I received from the incoming Chief changed everything.

"Michael," he said, "this has been a long time coming. As Chief, my first order of business is to get you hired. You've earned it. Congratulations."

Just like that, the process began again. No more blood thinners. No more friction at the top. But a few more hurdles remained. I had to retake the psych eval, redo the physical abilities test, and go back to the town's doctor's office, the same place where my dream had been crushed more than a decade earlier.

The shrink cleared me without hesitation. The physical test was a breeze. But the final appointment, the medical screening, that one rattled me.

I was sweating when I walked into that office. Anxious. This was the place where it all fell apart the first time. The male nurse who greeted me was from Danvers. He was upbeat, friendly. I liked him immediately. When he asked about my history, I shared the short version: Boston Marathon, a long road back, and a second chance. What I didn't share was that I had lost 80% of the hearing in my left ear during the blast. And the first test? Hearing.

I stepped into the soundproof booth, heart pounding. The ringing in my left ear was louder than ever in that silence. I wasn't even sure the test had started. I panicked. Raised my hand prematurely. Then came the real tones. Right ear, raise hand, again and again. Then silence. Too much silence. I raised my hand again, afraid I had missed a tone. This was it, I thought. It's over. I failed.

The nurse opened the door, puzzled. "Are you deaf?" he joked.

"I didn't know we'd started," I replied.

He smiled. "No worries." We moved on.

Next test: color vision. He pointed to a poster with two bars. "What colors are these?"

Damn. I'm colorblind.

No joke. Whenever those words come out of my mouth, "I'm colorblind," it always sets off the same routine. First the curiosity, then the questions, and eventually someone points at something and asks the one I hate the most: "What color is this?"

I call it the color game. And I hate the color game.

My eyes don't play by the same rules. I can see color, but I don't see it like you do. Sometimes my blues look purple. Sometimes my purples look blue. The lines blur, the shades cross, and what feels obvious to you becomes a guessing game for me.

I was doomed. I asked if I could get closer to the poster.

Ten years ago, the test was different, and I managed to fake my way through it. Not this time. When I hesitated, he caught on.

"Wait, are you colorblind?"

I hesitated again. He could see I wanted this. So did he.

He called an audible. The nurse handed me a book of color plates, those infamous multicolored circles with hidden numbers only visible if you can see color. We were off to a quick start. I got the first two.

"I see it, twelve!" I yelled, excited, and turned the page. My eyes locked on the next circle. I could see it.

"Nine," I said confidently.

Then nothing.

I failed the next eight. I knew it. He knew it. I hate the color game, and now it was standing between me and reaching this goal.

The nurse shrugged. "You got seven out of ten, not bad."

He wrote my fabricated score on the sheet.

That nurse was pulling for me. I'll never forget his kindness.

The rest of the appointment went smoothly. I passed every test. I left that office stunned. I had done it. Every box checked. Every barrier overcome. I went home and celebrated. Drinks, dinner, it was a perfect night.

But the celebration was short-lived...

The next day, I got a call from another nurse at the same office.

She told me there was an issue with the colorblind test. The 7 out of 10 I'd been credited with? It wasn't quite enough. Their standard required 8 to pass. I was one short.

I remember the quiet pause that followed. I didn't yell. I didn't beg. But I also didn't hold back. I was shocked we didn't have to talk about the hearing test, but I was honest. For nearly an hour, we stayed on the phone. I told her everything. Every step of this journey. From Orchard Street to Boylston Street and everything in between. The marathon. The aftermath. The struggle to be seen as whole again. I laid it all out.

Turns out, she could relate. Her son was in the process of applying to a local police department. He was physically strong, mentally sharp, and driven. But there was one part of the physical abilities test that kept tripping him up. He'd failed it. Twice. The department had given him one last shot. Next week. His dream was hanging by a thread, just like mine.

I think that conversation changed something for both of us.

Before we hung up, she scheduled me to come back into the office the very next day. "Ask for me when you get here," she said. I did exactly that.

When she brought me into the back room, I was clearly on edge. Hands sweaty. Heart pounding. This was it. My last shot. Everything came down to this.

We talked for about 15 minutes. She had a calm presence. A warmth about her. I could tell she wanted this to work out. Finally, she asked me to take a seat and rest my forehead against a viewfinder, one of those machines we all remember from gym class. The kind they use to test your vision.

I leaned in. Looked through the lenses. At first, nothing.

I panicked. Distinguishing LED lights is the hardest part of being colorblind. I thought, This is it. It's over.

She placed a hand on my shoulder, gently reassuring me. Her bedside, or that day's stoolside, manner was nothing short of amazing.

"Okay," she said softly. "I want you to look inside the machine and tell me the three colors you see."

Click.

Suddenly, the American flag appeared inside the viewfinder.

I took a breath. My heart caught in my throat. Then I smiled.

"Red, white, and blue."

I leaned back. She beamed. "See? I told you you could do it! Congratulations, Officer Chase!"

I laughed, part disbelief, part relief.

Unbeknownst to me, she had already told the entire office about my story before I even walked in. As soon as word got out I passed, people started pouring out of rooms I didn't even know existed. Staff from every corner of the office came to congratulate me. Hugs all around.

I turned to that sweet, 60-something-year-old nurse and said, "If it were socially acceptable, I'd kiss you on the mouth right now."

She burst out laughing. We all did.

That day, I officially passed. After more than a decade of setbacks, I had finally cleared the last hurdle.

I never found out if her son passed his test the following week. But I like to think he did. I hope he had a guardian angel with him that day, because I sure as hell had one with me.

15

Patrol

Between Sirens and Silence

When I graduated from the police academy, I couldn't wait to get started. Six months of classroom learning, drills, tactical training, case law, and pushups. All behind me. I was finally stepping into the job I had dreamed about since I was five years old. I'd be wearing the uniform, strapping on the duty belt, and sliding behind the wheel of a cruiser with my name on the roster.

But before you're on your own, you have to survive Field Training. Eight weeks riding with seasoned officers, learning how things really work when the pages of the textbook get replaced by screaming voices on the radio and unpredictable decisions at midnight.

I was lucky. I got paired with some of the best on the Danvers Police Department: Steven MacDonald, Eric Clarizia, and Justin Ellenton. These guys knew the job, knew the town, and most importantly, knew how to teach. Riding in a two-man car is like being locked in a rolling classroom where the curriculum changes by the minute. One call you're solving a neighbor dispute, the next you're clearing a house with a weapon potentially inside. In between, you're laughing about the insanity of the last call, sharing funny stories about your kids or telling old war stories from the job or the halls of the alt school.

Danvers is a small town on paper, roughly 28,000 residents, but during the day, that number swells to over 100,000 with the influx of workers, shoppers, and students. With major highways running through it, Danvers is a strange mix of quiet suburbia and steady activity. From a policing perspective, it's the perfect balance. There's just enough action to stay sharp, and just enough peace to catch your breath between calls.

I loved the job. The rhythm of the evening shift, the unpredictability, and the connection with the community. It just felt right.

Some of my most memorable moments came in unexpected ways.

One winter night, I was cruising through a quiet neighborhood when I saw an elderly woman, easily in her 80s. She was out shoveling her driveway. Well, more like *greeting the snow*. She was bundled up, but in a short jacket and a nightgown! She also wore rubber boots, red mittens, and a stocking cap, practically catching the first flakes as they landed.

I stopped to check in. I had my shovel, as I typically would bring along if snow was in the forecast.

She smiled and told me, "The snow gets too heavy if you wait. Gotta get it early."

That night, I shoveled her driveway. And I kept coming back whenever the snow fell, sometimes during patrol, sometimes after my shift. She always offered fresh baked goods in return. Whether it was cookies, banana bread, or muffins, it was always hard to say no. That driveway became a regular stop on snowy nights. And she became a quiet reminder of why this job mattered.

But not every night ended with banana bread.

There were overdoses. Domestics. Child abuse. Gun calls. Home invasions. The kind of stuff you never forget.

One night, I got dispatched to a hotel pool for a drowning. I sprinted through the parking lot and over to the pool, praying the caller was wrong. The child survived. But that panic, that helpless sprint toward something you can't control, it stayed with me.

And then there were the wild ones.

I'll never forget Sunday, September 8th, 2019. It was opening night of the NFL season. Patriots vs. Steelers. The banner had been raised. Brady was back. I picked up a quiet overtime shift thinking I'd stream the game from my cruiser and get paid to watch the GOAT do what he does.

I packed wings, popcorn, and a few other snacks, not exactly heart-healthy, but I was ready. Some of the guys on shift planned to meet back at the station to watch. I was going to head that way prior to half time, but I had parked near the high school. Pats streaming on the phone. Game time.

Then came the call: 30 year old male - abdominal pain.

Routine.

Until it wasn't.

I showed up to find firefighters waving me down, wide-eyed. "Chase! First floor. Guy's on the ground with a knife!"

They'd made entry but quickly retreated when they saw the weapon. I moved past them and announced myself.

"This is Officer Chase with the Danvers Police Department."

From inside the apartment, I could hear moaning. The door was cracked open just enough to be unsettling. I pushed it gently and stepped inside.

There he was. Lying on the floor. Shorts pulled down below his knees, covered in blood, holding a small folding knife.

"Drop the knife," I said.

He did, thankfully.

He was panicked and mumbling, trying to explain himself. Through the chaos, I pieced it together: he believed an ingrown pubic hair had started in his scrotum... and was now working its way up toward his heart. So he figured he'd cut it out himself.

Right there. On the floor. In the middle of his dining room.

He kept reaching for the self-induced wound, trying to dig his thumb and index finger in. I told him to stop. He didn't. I told him again. Still nothing.

So I told him I was going to cuff him to the table.

Not to arrest him, just to keep his hands off his own anatomy.

"We need a professional," I told him. "The attacking hair is not going to be removed from your dining room floor tonight."

I convinced him there was a specialist at the local Emergency Room who handled this sort of thing. It may have been a lie, but to my surprise, that little fib landed.

When the gurney came in, he jumped up, pulled his shorts back on, and hustled to the ambulance like we were heading to Foxboro for kickoff. It was a win.

After he was transported, I went back in and found the rest. A spoon, rubber ties, the usual clues that made everything else click into place.

Back in my cruiser, I took a long breath. Somewhere, Tom Brady was launching a touchdown pass to Julian Edelman. And I was filing a report on a guy who tried to remove his own testicle to save his heart.

This job will humble you. It'll crack you up. It'll break your heart and fill it all in one shift.

But I never stopped loving it.

There was another one that came while I was still in field training, so it was within the first eight weeks of me starting my career.

A woman called to report that her ex-husband had broken into her home with a shotgun. She believed he was still inside. She'd escaped. She was terrified.

We raced there. The lights, sirens, adrenaline pumping. The house was a small ranch with a basement.

After clearing the main level, I stepped toward the basement door. I was ready. Tactically sound. Focused. We had trained for this.

I looked at my FTO (Field Training Officer), Steve MacDonald, and nodded.

Before entering opening the basement door, he stopped me with a hand on my shoulder.

We both knew someone could be sitting at the bottom of that open staircase, weapon aimed up, waiting.

He leaned in close, and I braced for a lesson from his two decades on the job.

Instead, he whispered:

"You're only making 30 bucks an hour. You shoulda stayed at the school."

It was perfect.

It broke the tension, cleared the tunnel vision, and reminded me we were still human. We went down. We cleared the basement. No suspect. But the moment stuck with me.

This job is about more than bravery. It's about balance. About knowing when to be serious, and when to lighten the weight pressing on your chest.

After a few years on patrol, I started to feel a pull in a new direction. Not away from the work, just deeper into it.

A position opened up: School Resource Officer at Essex North Shore Agricultural and Technical School.

It wasn't about stepping back. It was about stepping in. Into a place where I could make a difference *before* the trauma, *before* the overdose, *before* the court date.

In just a few years being a street cop I had seen enough to know that the problems don't start with the crime. They start earlier. They begin with broken trust, broken homes, broken hearts. If I could be the adult a kid trusted *before* everything went sideways, maybe I could change the outcome entirely.

So I applied.

And that's where everything changed.

16

Back to School

Where the Badge Becomes the Bridge

I never left patrol because I was tired of the work. I left because I believed I could make a bigger impact somewhere else.

After several years on the road chasing chaos, shoveling snow for elders, talking people down from the edge, I started to realize that some of the calls that haunted me the most didn't start the night we got dispatched. They started long before. The overdose began with broken trust. The domestic started with unmet needs. The violence often began in a classroom years earlier, where a kid felt unheard, unseen, and unknown.

I still believed in the badge. I still believed in the job. But I believed even more in the idea that the earlier we show up for someone, the better chance we have to change their story.

That's when the opportunity came up: School Resource Officer at Essex North Shore Agricultural and Technical School.

The timing felt right. I had worked in education before, fifteen years with high school students who faced enormous challenges. I had coached high school soccer since 2001. I knew their language. I knew their walls.

And I knew how to break through them without force.

I also knew that the uniform can be a wall too, or a bridge. And I wanted to be the kind of cop who helped students see a badge and feel safe, not scared.

So I applied.

I wasn't the only one. Eight other officers put in for the position. Some had more than twenty years on the job. Others had only a few more years than me. But none of them had what I had: years inside the classroom, in the hallways, and on the sidelines. I knew that if I could just get into the interview room, I had a real shot.

The panel was a mix of senior members of my department and the school's administration. I spoke to my strengths: building relationships with students others struggled to reach, sitting in on countless educational meetings and trainings, and understanding school culture in a way most officers couldn't. I was the one candidate who could see school safety and policing through the eyes of an educator.

What I didn't realize until then was that all those years when I thought my dream of being a cop was slipping away, I had actually been building the foundation for this job. I wasn't stuck in the school when my life felt like it was falling apart. I was preparing for the next stage of it.

It was meant to be.

The first few days were an adjustment. I traded late-night patrols for morning announcements. My calls for service included vape pens, teenage heartbreak, and hallway arguments. On the surface, it might have looked like I had stepped down, trading the chaos of the street for the drama of a high school hallway.

But I learned quickly that this was not a step back. It was a step deeper.

Because beneath the everyday noise, the real calls came. Child sexual exploitation. Rapes and sexual assaults. Domestic abuse that followed kids into the building. Overdoses. Student suicides. Even kill lists scribbled in notebooks and shared with others.

I realized schools carry every story, both light and dark. Some days it is a vape pen in the bathroom. Other days it is a crisis that changes a life forever. My job was not just to show up when it happened. My job was to be present enough every day that kids knew they could come to me before it happened.

Being a School Resource Officer isn't about enforcement. It's about connection. You're part counselor, part coach, part crisis responder, part social worker. You build relationships one lunch table at a time, one fist bump in the hallway, one hard conversation after a kid makes a bad decision and needs to be reminded of their worth, not just their mistake.

And what made the transition even more powerful? I was back in a school.

But not just any school.

The first time I pulled into Essex Tech, I thought I had ended up at a college campus. Not just in size, but in spirit. It was massive. Still is. I used to joke that if you blindfolded me and dropped me in a random corner of campus, I might never find my way back to my office. That's not an exaggeration. It's 160 acres of opportunity, and most days it feels like a small city.

Nearly 2,000 people on campus. Students, staff, and visitors. There's a restaurant open to the public. A fully operational auto shop. A vet clinic that serves actual clients. A riding arena for our equine science students. I've watched kids run chainsaws, pour concrete, and operate heavy machinery before lunch.

It's a school, yes, but it functions more like an ecosystem.

What makes it even more unique is the staff. Half of them didn't come through traditional teacher training. They came from industry. Electricians, chefs, arborists, mechanics, cosmetologists, HVAC techs, and professionals who lived the work and now pour that knowledge into teenagers hungry to learn. They arrive without training in IEPs or classroom management, but they bring something just as valuable:

experience. Passion. A willingness to figure it out as they go.

Families prepare years in advance for a shot at Essex Tech. Some start as early as sixth grade, mapping out the path in hopes their child will be one of the lucky 500 selected from over 1,500 applicants. Some students ride the bus for hours every day just to get here. Because this place? It can change everything.

I've watched it happen.

Freshmen walk in unsure, overwhelmed, unaware of what's ahead. Four years later, they're licensed, working in co-ops, accepted into Ivy League schools, or landing jobs in high-end kitchens. Whether it's welding or animal science, culinary arts or carpentry, they find something here. Something that matters. Something that sticks.

Essex isn't just a place you attend. It's a place that transforms you.

And walking those halls again reminded me of what I loved about education. It's the energy, the collective mission, the feeling of being part of a team that shows up together every day to solve hard problems and support kids through the most critical years of their lives. Teachers, counselors, and support staff. We all had different titles, but the same goal: help these students grow into something more.

There's nothing like the energy inside a school building the day before a long weekend or school vacation. You can feel it in the air. The laughter, chaos, anticipation, joy. Where else do adults and kids get to experience that kind of countdown together? Where else do the entire staff and student body launch into summer break at the same moment?

That kind of shared experience creates something rare.

It creates a community.

And the longer I stayed in this role, the more I started to notice something deeper happening: students began to open up. Not just about the little stuff. About real things. The kind of things they don't share unless they believe you're safe.

One student came to my office and told me he didn't think he would live to see eighteen. Another told me he hadn't eaten that day. Others told me about abuse, addiction, divorce, pregnancy, loneliness. Some had no trusted adult in their lives. Not at home, not at school, not anywhere.

And that's when the question started ringing louder in my head:

How do we make sure every kid has someone?

Not just someone who can step in after the damage is done, but someone who can show up before the pain turns into something dangerous.

That question became my mission.

I didn't know it yet, but those hallway conversations, those tears in my office, and those fist bumps would eventually grow into something much larger. They would become the foundation for a schoolwide movement. A framework. A mission.

They would become Kindness Week.

They would become T/A Connect, The Trusted Adult Initiative.

But it all started here.

17

One Week. One Mission.

From Finish Line Smoke to Hallway Hope

It started in a meeting.

Just another sit-down with administrators, talking about our school's five-year strategic plan. Bullet points on a screen. Goals for the future. One of them stuck with me: Improve school culture.

It wasn't the first time I'd heard those words. Every school wants a better culture. Every school talks about climate. But this time felt different.

The principal and superintendent were both in their first year. So was I. None of us had a blueprint, but we had the same heart. We believed in kids. We believed in each other. And we believed that culture wasn't going to change because of a poster on a wall, it was going to change because we did something about it.

After that meeting, my wheels started turning.

What would it look like to create something real? Something that connected staff and students in a way that felt authentic, not scripted? Something that made the culture shift from the inside out?

Then it hit me: One Boston Day.

A way to honor the strength, resilience, and kindness that followed the darkest moment I had ever lived through. A way to tell my story. Not for sympathy, but for purpose. A way to remind students that they have power. That their small actions can ripple wide. That kindness, when done right, leaves a mark that outlasts everything else.

And so, in 2018, Kindness Week was born.

We scheduled it for the week leading up to April vacation, the same week as the Boston Marathon. It would be our way of turning tragedy into action. Grief into growth. Pain into purpose.

But I didn't want it to be gimmicky. These were high school students. They can smell fake from a mile away. I wanted it to be real.

Each year begins with an assembly just for the freshmen. I take the mic, and I walk them through what happened at the finish line. The smoke, the screams, the silence that followed. And then I tell them about what came next. The strangers who became heroes, the city that chose healing, the community that rallied around one simple truth: we're stronger when we're kind.

I introduce them to One Boston Day. I explain what it means to choose kindness, not as an act, but as a mindset. I give them examples. Real ones. Hold a door. Take out the trash without being asked. Make your bed. Write a thank-you card. Call your grandparents. Help your parents. Volunteer.

Kindness isn't complicated.

It's just forgotten.

All we need is a nudge. A reminder to push it from the back of our minds to the front.

And from there? It grew.

Each year, students started stepping up. They wanted to be involved, not because they had to, but because it felt good to be part of something bigger than themselves.

We started hosting a 5K and raised thousands of dollars for students who couldn't afford boots, tools, or other campus essentials. We took the Polar Plunge and raised even more. We hosted staff vs. student games. We read to elementary students. We helped food service deliver lunches. We helped facilities clean windows and pick up the cafeteria.

One year, our auto clinic repaired a donated vehicle. They got it running, detailed it, and gifted it to a single mother who needed a car to get to work and support her family. That wasn't a photo op. That was kindness in motion. That was Essex Tech at its best.

We brought in guest speakers. We celebrated our community. We gave back.

Staff and students. Together.

And in doing so, we gave new meaning to One Boston Day.

We didn't just remember what happened. We responded to it. With action, with unity, with kindness.

That was the heart of it all.

Not just honoring the past. But building something better because of it.

And I didn't know it then, but those acts, the ones that lit up our campus each April were also laying the foundation for something much bigger. Kindness Week wasn't the end of the story.

It was the beginning.

I started to notice something in the midst of all the giving:

Some students were doing everything they could to pour kindness into the world... while quietly running on empty themselves. They were surrounded by people but still felt alone. And as powerful as Kindness Week was, I knew we needed something more permanent. Something that lasted longer than a week and reached the kids who didn't know how to ask for help.

That's when I realized:

Kindness isn't enough if no one knows you well enough to notice when you're struggling.

And that's when the real question hit me:

Who do our kids turn to when they need someone?

That question would become the foundation for the next chapter of my work.

A question that didn't just need an answer, it needed a plan.

18

The Missing Piece

How Do We Make Sure Every Kid Has Someone?

It started as a whisper. A question that wouldn't leave me alone.

How do we make sure every kid has someone?

I asked it after a student sat in my office and told me he didn't think he'd live to see eighteen. I asked it after another admitted he hadn't eaten in two days. I asked it when kids cried in front of me, told me they had no one. No trusted adult at home, no trusted adult at school, and no plan for what to do when the weight of life got too heavy.

Over time, that question stopped being a whisper. It became a mission.

I had spent nearly two decades in education, and I've sat in more student support meetings than I can count. Meetings with six, eight, sometimes a dozen professionals in the room. Each with a laptop, and packet of notes on the kid. We'd talk and talk. We'd hypothesize. We'd build plans based on what we thought the student needed. Then we'd revise the plan when it didn't work. And we'd start again.

All that time. All that expertise. All that salary.

And yet, far too few of those adults ever did the most obvious thing: Ask the kid.

Ask them what's wrong. Ask them what they need. Ask them who they trust. Ask them how we can help. Then shut up. Listen. Let them lead you.

That's where T/A Connect began.

Not in a boardroom. Not on a whiteboard. In a hallway. In a lunchroom. In the quiet space between crises. In the relationships we weren't measuring but were changing everything.

T/A Connect - The Trusted Adult Initiative - started as an experiment. What if we just asked students who they trust? What if we used that data to create real connection points? What if we stopped guessing and started listening?

So we built the survey. Simple, direct, honest. Who are your trusted adults at school? Who are your trusted adults at home?

Who do you go to when life gets hard? Who listens without judgment?

The answers were powerful.

Sometimes heartbreaking.

We found students who didn't have a single adult they felt safe with. We found staff who had no idea how much they meant to certain students. We found patterns. Some encouraging and some alarming.

But more than anything, we found our starting point.

From there, we built out the initiative. Identified a team of adults at each school called T/A Liaisons -trusted, present, steady. Staff who could be trained, empowered, and elevated as go-to supports for students in need. We started training staff on how to build real relationships with hard-to-reach kids. We offered professional development, not just on pedagogy or compliance, but on human connection.

Because here's the truth:

Every school shooter leaves behind signs. Every suicide has a silent build-up. Every act of violence has a timeline that started long before it exploded.

And at almost every turn, the missing piece is the same:

No trusted adult.

T/A Connect isn't a magic wand. But it's a damn good question: Who do our students trust?

And what are we doing with that information?

Because the answer to that question is the difference between a student reaching out, or disappearing. Between someone breaking down, or breaking through.

T/A Connect doesn't fix kids. It doesn't fix schools.

It gives them something to build on.

And in a world that feels increasingly disconnected, that might be the most important thing we can offer.

It all started with one question.

How do we make sure every kid has someone?

Now, we're finally answering it.

19

The Quiet Hero

A Stepdad, Veteran, and a Blueprint For Love

It started with a casual hello. A man coming to pick up my mom. The first date she'd gone on since the divorce. Nothing serious, just dinner. But he kept coming around. And little by little, the door to our family cracked open, and Jim didn't kick it down. He didn't ask for anything. He didn't try to win anyone over. He just waited, showed up, and stayed.

Jim had three kids of his own, but you'd never know it by how he treated my brother and me. He didn't differentiate, didn't compare. He just *loved*. Quietly, steadily, like he had all the time in the world for us to figure it out. And eventually, we did.

He wasn't the kind of man who needed to prove anything. That's what made him so damn easy to trust. Jim had this sixth sense, a rare gift for knowing when to step in and when to step back. Some days he'd offer a word, a nod, or just stand nearby. Other days, he'd let me come to him, knowing the moment had to be mine to initiate. That kind of patience? That kind of presence? It's the stuff fatherhood is supposed to be built on.

Jim never raised his voice. Not once. After years of chaos and noise in the house I grew up in, his silence was powerful. It wasn't the absence of sound, it was the presence of peace. He created a new kind of home. One where dinners weren't just about eating. They were about *gathering*. They were about showing up and staying awhile.

If there's a smell that defines my childhood post-divorce, it's the simmer of Jim's red sauce. No one knows the full recipe. It's sacred. Protected. Earned. And standing next to him at the stove, stirring that sauce, felt like being let into a secret society. Not of cooks. Of *belonging*.

Sundays became sacred. Not because of church, but because of football. My brother, Makena, our families, we all showed up. It was the rhythm of the fall. Laughter, food, storytelling, trash talk. And Jim at the center of it all, anchoring the table, the kitchen, the home.

But the thing about Jim is... he's more than a great stepdad, more than a cook, more than a man who brought peace to a house that badly needed it. He's a veteran. A man who served our country in Vietnam and never bragged about it once.

Jim saw things no man should see. Heard cries no one should hear. Got shot in the leg and carried the scar with quiet dignity. But he didn't just carry that pain, he *used* it. He turned trauma into wisdom. War into perspective. Pain into purpose.

He never forced those stories on me. But when I was ready, when *I* needed him, he shared. After Boston, when my world had gone sideways and I couldn't find my footing, it was Jim who helped me stand back up. He didn't try to fix me. He didn't tell me to get over it. He just sat with me in the dark and told me he knew what it was like. He told me I wasn't alone.

That's what love looks like. That's what being a father is.

Jim never had to be any of those things for me. He chose to be. That's what makes it so powerful. That's what makes it real. He showed me that biology has nothing to do with fatherhood. Showing up, listening, holding steady when the storm comes, that's what matters.

As I raise my own daughter, as I try to give Makena a home that's filled with laughter, safety, and Sunday sauce, I think of Jim. I think of the legacy he's left in the quietest, most powerful way possible. He didn't come into our lives with a bang. He didn't need to.

He came in with a whisper, and it changed everything.

That whisper echoes now in how I love today.

I'm in a relationship with an incredible woman named Casey. She's funny, fiery, patient, and loyal in ways that stop me in my tracks. She's not just my partner, she's my best friend. She's restored my faith in love, in marriage, in second chances. She's helped me grow, made me a better communicator, a better father, a better man.

She's also a phenomenal mother to two amazing kids: Mia, age six, and Chase, age eight. Chase is on the autism spectrum. When we first got close, Casey shared her fears. fears every strong single mother carries. Would anyone love not just her, but her whole world? Would Chase be too much for someone to take on?

But the truth is, Chase wasn't going to scare me away. He never could. I've spent years working in special education. I've sat in rooms with kids who couldn't find the words. I've celebrated their smallest victories and stood by them through their toughest days. I didn't know it back then, but I was unknowingly preparing for Chase the moment I walked through the doors at Northshore Academy.

And now? We're close...*really* close. Chase is funny, loving, persistent, and endlessly curious. He has a brain that fascinates me. He's a prankster with a huge heart, a walking contact list who remembers every phone number he's ever seen. He repeats things, busts chops, and fills every room with energy. I feel his love every single day. I know I'm in his heart because he's so clearly in mine.

Then there's Mia. That kid is the definition of fun. She's athletic, artistic, kind, and protective of her brother in a way that reminds me of Brad when we were growing up. She's tough and smart and so far ahead of her years that I joke she's already someone's future best college roommate - loyal, witty, and just plain cool to be around.

I love them both with all my heart. As if they were my own.

None of this would have been possible without Jim. He gave me the blueprint. He taught me that family isn't something you inherit. It's something you build. And now I get to build one with Casey, with Makena, with Mia, and with Chase.

And when the time comes, I'll ask Casey to marry me. I already know my answer. Because I've already made the choice Jim once made for me.

To show up.

To love quietly.

To stay.

"Love you, man." - Jim Kelleher

20

Fatherhood & Purpose

The One Thing That Held Me Steady

Some people talk about anchors. The things that keep them grounded when life gets stormy. I've had a few over the years: my work, my calling, the people who believed in me when I couldn't believe in myself. But no anchor has ever held as steady, as firm, or as fiercely as my daughter, Makena.

Makena wasn't just a light in my life, she was the lighthouse. Always there, always shining, always pulling me back to shore when the waves got too big. There were moments, especially after the bombing, when I felt like I might drift too far. When the pain, the trauma, and the noise of the world started closing in. But even in those moments, I could still see her. I could still hear her laugh. Still remember the way her tiny hand used to wrap around my finger like she was hanging on for dear life. Though, truthfully, it was me doing the hanging on.

The moment she arrived changed everything. She was born at Beverly Hospital, and I got to push her, only minutes old, in one of those little plastic baby trays, down the hallway from the operating room to the nursery. She had her tiny hospital hat on and was wrapped in those standard-issue blankets, but to me, she looked like royalty. I followed the nurse's lead through swinging double doors, completely unaware of where I even was in the hospital. I couldn't think. I couldn't speak. I could only focus on her. She was my little miracle that had just arrived.

What I didn't know was that the entire extended family was waiting on the other side of those doors. And when I came through, overcome with emotion, I choked out the words, "Meet Makena!" That's all I could manage with the tears streaming down my face, voice cracking, heart exploding. Brad still tells the story to this day about how I was a babbling mess. He does a full reenactment with hands flailing, fake tears, voice cracking dramatically, and a stutter. It's quite the performance. A loving roast. And every single year on Makena's birthday, and plenty of times in between, he brings it out again. It's become a tradition, a reminder, a celebration of the day I received the greatest gift of my life.

After the divorce, something powerful happened, Makena chose to live with me full time. That decision, at her age (16), said everything. It wasn't just about where she wanted to sleep or which house had her favorite snacks. It was about trust. It was about love. It was about knowing where her emotional home really was. And I've never taken that for granted.

Especially in the years since the divorce, we've built something together. Something that goes beyond the traditional idea of father and daughter. We're a team. We've created traditions, like our annual trip to a tropical destination. Just the two of us. Every year, for four or five days, we shut the world off and disappear into our own little oasis.

Those trips have become sacred. Airports and sunburns. Poolside laughs and fancy dinners. Fillets and coconut drinks. Quiet chats about life. Excursions to waterfalls, cliff jumping, snorkeling spots or zip line jungles. It's connection. Reconnection. Growth. Rest. It's where I get to see her heart on full display, curious, joyful, thoughtful. It's where we both exhale.

Makena doesn't just make me want to be better, she *makes* me better. Being her dad has been the greatest gift of my life. Not a day goes by that I don't feel that. Not a day where I don't thank God that I get to be her father. She's not just my daughter, she's my reminder that love is the strongest force in the world. Stronger than fear. Stronger than failure. Stronger than the worst day of my life.

When people ask me how I've managed to keep showing up, to keep pushing forward after all that I've seen and been through, I don't always have the words. But I see her face, and I know the answer. *It's Makena. It's always been Makena.*

From the time she was little, she's had this quiet strength. A kind of steady presence that doesn't need to shout to be felt. She leads with kindness. She's the one helping the kid sitting alone at lunch. The one defending someone who's being picked on. She has this rare gift. It's one I've seen in only a few people in my life - to make others feel safe just by being near them. And every time I see that in her, I realize she's been doing the same for me all along.

There's a moment I come back to often. I had just gotten home after a rough 16 hour shift at the police station. I was emotionally raw, exhausted, questioning everything. I walked in the door, and there she was. Sitting at the table, waiting, completely in her own world. She looked up, smiled, and said, "Hi, Dad. It's spa day!" And in that moment, everything I had been carrying dropped. All it took was her voice to remind me: *I'm home. I'm loved. I matter.* She did my makeup. Painted my nails. And then my favorite, a back massage. She's always been a pro. She tells me her hands a really strong from years of making slime on the living room floor. I guess it was good for something.

She doesn't know how many times she's saved me. I'm not sure she ever will. But this chapter, this part of the story, it's hers. Because every man has a moment in life when he realizes who he is. And for me, that moment came the day she was born. I wasn't just Michael Chase anymore. I was *Makena's dad.* And I still am. And I always will be.

She is, and always will be, the very best part of me.

And now, as I watch her grow into this strong, kind, resilient young woman, I'm not just proud, I'm in awe. She was my reason then. She's my reason now.

21

Sully

One Speed

Some people walk into a room and shift the energy. Sully didn't just shift it, he owned it. My cousin summed him up perfectly after meeting him at my wedding. "Sully's the kind of guy who walks in a room and every girl wants to marry and every guy wants as a best friend."

That was Sully.

The smile. The presence. The way he could light up a room without trying. He had a gift for making people feel like they mattered, and he used it constantly. He could win anyone over, and he did it without effort. It was just who he was. It wasn't calculated. It was him.

On paper, he was Matthew Francis Sullivan. Born and raised in Greensboro, North Carolina. College graduate. East Carolina University. Sales rep. Athlete. Son. Brother. Uncle. But that paper version doesn't touch who he really was.

Sully was movement. Energy. Chaos and compassion wrapped in the same package. He was the kind of friend who would call just to check in, then stay on the phone for hours, laughing, gaming, talking about nothing and everything.

We met at East Carolina University. From the start, we clicked. Some days at the apartment turned into hours of GoldenEye on the N64. The room filled with laughter, trash talk, and the occasional argument that always ended with another round. That was our crews version of bonding.

As we got older, life stretched the distance between us. He stayed in North Carolina, and I ended up in Boston, but it never mattered. We just swapped couches and barstools for headsets. Call of Duty became our meeting place. We talked about work, family, and life while we played. He was my daily constant. My best bud.

Then I realized I wasn't alone in calling him that.

At his funeral, the church was packed. Standing room only. People from everywhere. I met dozens of guys who said the same thing. "Sully was my best friend." How could that be? I thought he was mine. But that was the beauty of him. He had enough space in his heart for everyone. He made each person feel like they were the most important.

That kind of effort takes something out of you. It has to. Sully battled his own darkness. He struggled with anxiety and depression but still worked overtime to make sure everyone else was okay. He filled your cup even when his was empty.

That is what made him special, and what breaks my heart most when I think about him.

He lived life full throttle. If he loved something, he went all in. Working out. Ice cream. Video games. Everything he did was at max volume. He lived that way, and he rode that way too.

Sully loved motorcycles. The speed. The rush. The freedom. He would send me videos from his GoPro, flying down backroads at speeds that belonged to airplanes. I would yell at him, play the dad role, tell him to slow down. We all did. But Sully was Sully.

He crashed once and survived. Laid the bike down, slid off the road, banged up, but alive. I thought that would be it. I begged him to sell the bike, but he couldn't. It was part of him.

A few months later, he was back on it. Back with his crew. Back doing what he loved. That is when the call came. He had crashed again. This time, he didn't make it.

He was thirty-four.

Losing him felt like losing a piece of myself. It was one week after my birthday and less than a year after the Boston Marathon bombing. I was already trying to make sense of trauma, and then he was gone.

Sully had been one of my biggest supports after the bombing. He checked in constantly. Listened. Laughed when I needed it. Never said the wrong thing. He was just there. Solid. Present.

And then he wasn't.

Grief comes in waves, but the kind that comes for your best friend never really leaves. I can hear his laugh. See that grin. Feel that presence.

He lived his life the same way he loved his people, all in.

Sully taught me that friendship is not about time or proximity. It is about presence. About showing up, even when you are carrying your own weight. He was relentless in love and loyalty. I think about that every time I remind myself to be a better friend, a better father, a better man.

Be like Sully.

22

Magnet

The Pull Towards Purpose

It was the Fourth of July, 2024. Fireworks were waiting in the distance, but I never made it that far. I was in the passenger seat with Makena in the back, heading home from dinner with some of my college buddies. My friend Brandon Crocker, a retired FBI agent, was driving. Traffic had thinned just enough to feel easy. Then the lights ahead didn't look like fireworks anymore.

Two cars were scattered across the intersection like toys thrown by an angry child. One was on its side, the other crumpled with steam pouring from the hood. I told my buddy to pull over. We were out before the car stopped rolling.

He boosted me onto the overturned SUV. I used my elbow to shatter the rear window of the driver's side and reached in through a cloud of deployed airbags and dust. The driver hung in his seat belt, dazed. His wife was wedged against the road through the smashed passenger window, half in, half out. I cut the fabric of the airbag and spoke to both of them until help arrived.

When fire and EMS took over, I went to check the other car. A off duty nurse was kneeling beside the driver, trying to talk him through the pain. His legs were mangled, bones pressing against torn skin. He moved to his feet when I got there, moving on adrenaline. Then it hit him. His eyes rolled back and he collapsed. I slid in beside him and guided him to the ground. I started by giving several firm sternum rubs, but eventually needed to start compressions.

It was loud again. Sirens. Voices. Blood and smoke. Somewhere in the chaos, Makena was watching from the car. She's seen too much of this already. But I know she also saw what it looks like to lean in when most people freeze.

That's how this chapter starts, but it could have started anywhere.

Because this wasn't the first time. Not by a long shot.

A year before that, I was sitting at a bar in Hudson, Massachusetts. The kind of place where strangers become friends for the night. A couple sat beside me, already a few drinks deep but cheerful enough. A few bites into their dinner, the woman started choking. Her boyfriend froze, slapped my arm, eyes wide. He needed me.

She stood up, hands at her throat, the universal sign. The stool crashed backward and everyone around us just watched. I moved behind her, told her to cough, then started thrusts. Three. Nothing. I gave three back blows. Nothing. I readjusted and began thrusts again. Fourth. Nothing. Fifth. A piece of chicken the size of a golf ball shot across the bar.

She turned and hugged me. The man started crying. Everyone else still stood there like statues. It was a longest thirty seconds I can remember. Even after she sat down, people were still frozen. Fight, flight, or freeze. Most choose freeze.

June 2022. Daniella's Restaurant in Peabody. Same story, different scene.

A man celebrating his birthday stood to go to the restroom and dropped like a stone. One second upright, next second gone. I ran as he hit the ground. His girlfriend screamed. I rolled him to a recovery position, checked his pulse. He came to, dazed, confused. Said he felt fine. We moved him to a chair and that's when he started seizing.

I eased him to the floor again, kept his head safe, waited for help. The whole place fell silent except. The air felt heavy. The kind of moment that separates the ones who act from the ones who watch.

St. Patrick's Day in Portland, Maine. One of my favorite cities, one of my favorite bars. Two floors, plenty of laughter, and a staircase I'll never forget.

An intoxicated woman tried to make her way down the stairs and lost her footing. She tumbled the whole way, 14 steps, crashing into the wall at the bottom. The sound of her head hitting the hardwood cut through the music. I ran over. She was out cold, limp, blood pooling fast. I used a clean kitchen towel to hold pressure on her head and kept her neck still until the medics arrived. She came to, slurring, laughing even. Said she'd be back on the bar crawl before it ended. I didn't doubt her spirit, just her balance.

The owner gave me free drinks for the day. It was a very nice gesture on a busy holiday in the city.

Summer of 2021, Ossipee, New Hampshire. I was at Brad's lake house, grilling shirtless in a bathing suit when my buddy Mike Delisio, a Danvers firefighter, called. "Need you. Now."

I grabbed the first pair of shoes I saw and took off running down the dirt road. A side-by-side ATV had rolled over. A woman was trapped underneath, her son pacing in circles and still in shock. Her leg was crushed, bone visible, blood soaking into the gravel.

We lifted the ATV with help from neighbors and slid her out. The first young cop on scene looked terrified. I told him to call for a med flight. She was fading fast. Somehow, she made it. They saved her leg. That is a day everyone on scene will remember. Those memories don't go away.

There was the time on Route 16 in New Hampshire, heading home from the lake with Makena in the car. Two vehicles collided right in front of us. I watched them spin, metal twisting, glass exploding into sunlight. I parked sideways to block traffic, told Makena to stay put, and ran to help. Everyone was shaken, one dog was shaking worse than the people. I stayed until the troopers came. Makena stayed calm. She's built like her dad that way.

A month earlier, I was on Route 95 in Winchester, Massachusetts. Two cars, both totaled. I positioned my vehicle to shield the wreck and helped the drivers out. No one seriously hurt. Just stunned, confused faces, that familiar silence again.

Go back farther.

2004, Manchester, New Hampshire. I was working surveillance as a private investigator, sitting in a car, watching a suspect I thought was faking an injury for insurance money. Out of nowhere, a speeding car clipped a parked one and rolled three times, maybe four. I ran toward it, glass flying everywhere. The car landed upright, smoke pouring from the hood.

The driver was conscious. I talked to them through the broken window until help arrived. I remember how slow it all felt. How my hands didn't shake. How other people around me looked lost, like they didn't know which way gravity was pulling. I did.

2015, Route 1A in Wenham, Massachusetts. A car on its side, tires still spinning. I climbed up on top of it and peered through the window. The driver was hanging from the seatbelt, upside down, eyes darting, disoriented but alive. Smoke rose from under the hood. Neighbors came running. I stayed there, talking to the driver, until police and fire arrived.

Sometimes I wonder if these moments find me because I'm looking for them. Then I remember that most of the time, I'm not. I've been on boats, at bars, on back roads, even on vacation, and somehow the world keeps throwing me into chaos.

It's not about luck. It's not about heroism either. It's about being wired a certain way.

MAGNET

When things go bad, most people freeze. My switch flips the other direction. The noise drops out. The world slows down. I move toward it. Every time.

Maybe that's what a magnet does. It doesn't chase what it pulls toward. It just stays true to what it is.

So yeah, I guess that's me. A magnet. Not for fame or fortune. Not for danger either. I'm a magnet for moments that remind me why I'm here. Moments that strip life down to its most honest parts. People. Presence. Purpose.

And as strange as it sounds, I wouldn't change a thing.

23

Still Standing

Becoming Who You Were Meant to Be

There was a time I didn't think I'd ever sleep again. A time when the ringing in my ears drowned out everything else. A time when I could still feel the heat of the blast on my skin, still taste the iron, sulfur and smoke in the back of my throat. A time when I didn't know if the little girl I'd carried would live, or if I could.

But here I am. Still standing.

That day on Boylston Street changed everything. But so did the ones that came after.

The quiet ones. The ones no one sees. The early mornings when I laced up my boots and showed up anyway. The late nights at my desk wondering if anything I was doing actually mattered. The hard conversations. The harder silences. The days I wanted to quit. The days I almost did.

People sometimes ask me what the turning point was and when it all started to get better. And the truth is, there wasn't one. There were a thousand. A thousand tiny choices to keep going. To speak the truth. To reach for help. To hold my daughter's hand and let her laughter remind me that life was still good.

There's no single moment where the pain ends and the healing begins. It's messier than that. It's layered. It shows up uninvited and leaves in pieces. But over time, the pieces form something new. Something stronger.

I used to think the goal was to get back to who I was.

Now I know better.

The goal is to become who you're meant to be, because of what you've been through, not in spite of it.

I've stood on stages across the country, telling a story I never asked to carry. I've cried in front of strangers. I've hugged people I just met because they saw themselves in my pain. I've been asked, over and over again, what gives me the right to speak. And the answer is simple:

Nothing.

Nothing gives me the right.

Except maybe the fact that I keep showing up. That I tell the truth, even when it hurts. That I built something, not to impress anyone, but because I believe every student deserves someone who sees them. Because I believe relationships can save lives.

Because mine were saved by them.

By Brad and Jen. By Makena. By Jim. By Mom. By Dad. By Cindy. By Casey, and the kids. By the nurses and cops and teachers who didn't let go. By the athletes I coached and students that trusted me.

I still carry the weight. But I also carry the light.

The little boy who once imagined monsters invading from the sky is now a man who faced them in real life and ran toward the fire.

The guy who was told he'd never wear the badge found a way to put it on anyway.

The teacher who sat in restraint debriefs and wrote behavior plans is now on stage teaching educators how to build school cultures that heal.

And the dad who once whispered "Meet Makena" through a flood of tears is now watching her become everything good in this world.

So no, I don't have a neat ending to give you.

I'm still learning. Still falling short. Still rebuilding.

But I'm here.

Still listening. Still curious. Still trying. Still standing.

And maybe, just maybe, that's enough.

Not just for me. But for anyone who's ever wondered if they'd make it too.

Because if you're reading this, I want you to know:

You can.

You're not alone.

You're still standing too.

About the Author

Michael Chase is a cop, keynote speaker, and former educator who spent fifteen years working with students who often needed someone to believe in them.

He was standing less than fifteen feet from the second blast at the 2013 Boston Marathon and rushed toward the injured in the chaos that followed, an experience that changed the direction of his life.

Today, he shares his message of resilience, healing, and human connection with audiences across the country. His story has been featured on 20/20, honored by the Boston Celtics, and recognized for its impact in communities nationwide.

You can connect with me on:

🌐 https://www.michaelchasespeaks.com
𝐟 https://www.facebook.com/michael.chase.372683
🔗 https://www.instagram.com/michaelchasespeaks

www.ingramcontent.com/pod-product-compliance
Lightning Source LLC
Chambersburg PA
CBHW020945090426
42736CB00010B/1273